AF605048

What Readers are Saying

"Live Wide Awake" - what a great book for every age and maturity level! The author does a wonderful job creating an environment in which you can dig deeper, gain wisdom, and deepen your spiritual walk with God. Through her personal antidotes, thought-provoking questions, and daily activities for further reflection, Laura helps you learn to think outside the box.

You won't look at the scriptures the same again - grab your copy, grab one for your sisters, your mother, your daughters, and your friends! Choose to open your eyes and your heart, letting the Word resonate in your life - Living Wide Awake!

BRENDA ROSER

I absolutely loved it! Laura tells great stories that relate so well to all of us, stories that are honest, true, raw, and compelling. The daily practices are creative, interactive, and challenging. I loved being directed to write down my thoughts about a passage one day, and the next I would read aloud so I could be listening to God's word and seeing how it impacted my day/week. Live Wide Awake challenged me to spend more time with Jesus and the more time I spent with him, the more time I wanted to be at His feet, in the Word, and prayer.

GWEN EBBERS

Live Wide Awake encouraged, instructed, and helped me to converse with Jesus, to see Jesus on a more personal level. He already knows everything about me. When I quiet myself and sit in God's presence, my awareness of Him in my life is greater. I loved how this book encouraged me to journal, self-examine, and fall deeper in love with my Abba Father. And for that, I am so grateful.

JULIE SCHROTENBOER

I love the rhythm of the book, the time to hang with small amounts of Scripture, and all the personal intro's to each day. Stories are told in intimate ways that invite me in. Laura is kind to herself and to all those she mentions, honoring the stories with grace for everyone.

KP FAGRE

Laura is good at creating word pictures for the reader that draws them into the story she is telling. I just absolutely loved her description of Mother Mary! It made me feel as though I've known her all of my life. One of my favorite stories was about Laura's dog, Moses. Animals are a tender spot for me. I loved the coming back around for the one well-timed sentence: "You want Moses to know that all good things come from his *Master*". I also like the creative way the chapters are set up.

RHONDA MOORE

I enjoyed all of the personal stories. I also enjoyed the Presence Prayer; wondering questions, repetition, thinking about sitting face to face with Jesus and talking with Him, reading in multiple translations. These were all great ways to engage with the Word and keep my devotional time fresh and active.

SUSAN RINGEON

LIVE WIDE AWAKE

LAURA DEGROOT

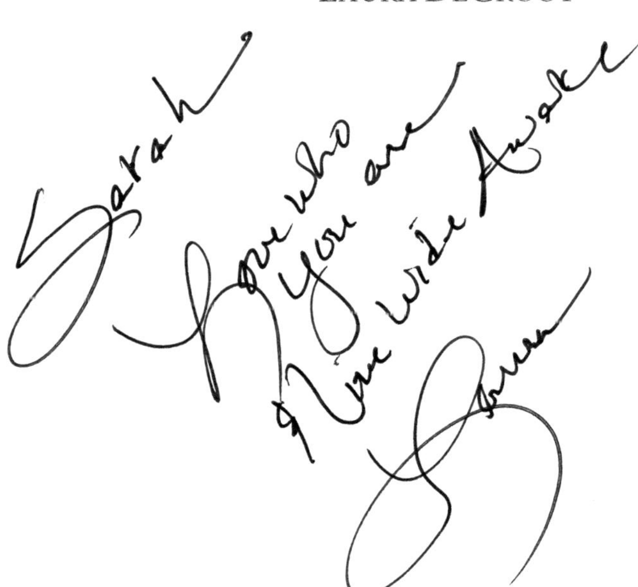

Copyright © 2019 Laura DeGroot

All rights reserved. No part of this publication may be reproduced, distributed, or transmitted in any form or by any means, including photocopying, recording, or other electronic or mechanical methods, without the prior written permission of the publisher, except in the case of brief quotations embodied in reviews and certain other non-commercial uses permitted by copyright law.

Inside book artwork by April Bowen, Betel Box Design
Instagram: @Betelboxdesign

ISBN: 978-1-7345827-0-3

A NOTE ABOUT TRANSLATIONS OF THE BIBLE

In this book, any scripture that is written out will come from the New Living Translation unless otherwise noted. I have used the NLT since I read through the Bible in one year in that translation, finding the wording to be similar to the way I normally speak and hear others speak. Eugene Peterson said that Jesus spoke the language of God in the language of men and women. The language of the Bible, especially the New Testament, was written in street language, the plain and simple way ordinary people talked.

"Scriptures are liveable - that God's word is personal address, inviting, commanding, challenging, rebuking, judging, comforting, directing - but not forcing. Not coercing. We are given space and freedom in these biblical pages to answer, to enter into the conversation. More than anything else the Bible invites our participation in the work and language of God." Eugene Peterson[1]

I will suggest several times you read or listen to the scriptures from multiple translations or paraphrases. If you've been a Bible reader, studier, or investigator for years, you run into what I call familiarity fog. You read something for the tenth time or fifty-fifth time and because it's so familiar-sounding, even if you don't understand what you're reading, you tend to skim and forget. By listening or reading a different translation, you see and hear something new. The chance for insight or question-asking is more likely.

I will often suggest reading *The Message* because it saved me from getting lost, getting bored, and getting on with my life without reading the Bible. I began as a closet reader. Somewhere I got my hands on an Old Testament, Psalms and Proverbs version of The

Message. I didn't tell anyone I was reading it, because there were people who seemed to look down on this paraphrase for reasons I didn't understand. But for the first time, I felt like I was hearing what the Living Word had to say. I was understanding, and getting excited to go back and read more. Eventually, my experience reading *The Message* became something I shared. Years later, I learned about Eugene Peterson the translator, and years after that, I got to meet this genuine, wise, compassionate man and his wife in person at a small gathering for a weekend in Colorado. He was a Greek and Hebrew professor turned pastor. After years of being a pastor, he became aware of how people didn't care much, didn't read much, didn't know much about the Bible. He wanted people to wake up to the "beauty and hope that connects with our real lives." He started to lead others to approach Scripture with this question: "What does it mean and how can I live it?"[2]

One of the reasons I wrote Live Wide Awake was for the same reason Eugene Peterson wrote *The Message*, to invite people to live from their true authentic self, toward their whole self by engaging with the Living Words of God. I want people to read, listen, pay attention, respond, and be transformed in contrast to reading the Bible for gathering information. That is my personal experience with *The Message* and why I suggest you use it as a source of your engagement with God's story.

Eat This Book by Eugene Peterson is a recommended read if you're interested in learning more about the history of translations and paraphrases of the Bible. *Living By the Book* by Howard G. Hendricks and William D. Hendricks has a helpful appendix of 25 Bibles and a brief description of each. Each of those books has informed my own engaging with God's story.

DEDICATION

In memory of my dad Andy Ploegstra, aka Mr. Wonderful, who told me I had to write, and his voice was the one I finally listened to. He also told me that I didn't have to be a great writer, because other people would be able to take what I said and make it better.

With deep gratitude to those who not only made it better but actually made it happen by reading, re-reading, engaging, correcting, asking questions and suggesting: Mary Ploegstra, Lauren VanKlaveren, Lyndsay DeGroot, Adie Johnson, Heidi Hoback, Angela Hansen, Kim Haggerty, Lori Jonker, Amanda Jones, and Sarah Boonstra. Thank you for speaking encouraging words all along the way. Bless you people.

To my writing coach Lise Cartwright for laughing at me and with me and telling me what to do all of which was remarkably helpful.

To Hopewriters for providing a community for any writer no matter stage they're in. Thank you for tools, training, Tuesday Teaching, and normalizing the odd and wonderful life of writing.

In honor of my mother Mary Ploegstra who prayed over me and encouraged me to finish strong what I started. She still believes in her wildflower girl. And this wildflower girl loves her so.

With humble yet humongous thanks to my hubby JR who sees all, hears all, bears almost all that comes with the journey of writing, and who attends to my extra-neediness in kind and generous ways.

JR, whose sexy smiling photo sits on my writing desk, the only distraction I don't mind. I love you forever.

With gratitude to Lauren VanKlaveren (aka Thing Two), who asked me to finish this book because she wanted a gift to give people and I know of no greater gift than that of the Good News of Jesus who loves us like crazy. Bless you for keeping so many things organized and orderly and dealing with details. I love you tremendously.

With a toast to Lyndsay DeGroot (aka Thing One), who never ceased to tell me to finish writing the book before I did the next thing. And for sharing writing tools and hacks as she too writes all the words for her dissertation. She has championed me as a writer as long as I can remember. I love you ginormously.

And most importantly,

For you, Jesus my Master, Abba Father, Holy Spirit.
You can have 'all of me.'

Table of Contents

Introduction

I want everyone to know God.

I know plenty of people who don't have any interest in God. I know plenty of people who know *about* God. And I know people who truly *know* God. I know this is true: God is knowable, and He wants everyone to know Him. A powerful, ongoing, transformative way of knowing God personally is by meditating on his Living Word--the inspired words that were often first spoken, then written down poetically, historically, narratively, and instructionally in books, chapters, verses, and letters.

You've read those words before, right? Or no, maybe you haven't. Maybe you've tried. Maybe you did a few years ago, but they didn't do anything for you. Maybe you never knew where to start. That's fair. I hear you. I completely understand.

Getting to know God through His Word takes more than just reading the text. It takes listening. It takes reading over and over and over again. It takes deep digging, learning to ask questions, living in the questions. Getting to know God through His Word requires reading out loud, observing details in the passage, outlining, list-making, using your imagination and responding to what you're hearing. Drawing, singing, painting, dancing, songwriting, and walking in nature are other creative ways to engage with the Creator. The point is, getting to know God through His word is active, not passive.

> *"For the Word of God is alive and powerful. It is sharper than the sharpest two-edged sword, cutting between soul and spirit, between joint and marrow. It exposes our innermost thoughts and desires. Nothing in all of creation is hidden from God. Everything is naked and exposed before his eyes, and he is the one to whom we are accountable." Hebrews 5:12*

My friend Adie always reminds me that Scripture is meant to be informational and formational. When we interact with Scripture, it needs to move beyond intellectual knowledge. When we allow the Word of truth to sink into our hearts--our will, the center of our being--we are transformed to become more and more like what God intended us to become.

If you find a fantastic restaurant, read a brilliant book, or hear an inspiring speaker, song, or sermon, you are likely going to share that with someone else. At the end of each chapter, you are similarly invited to share what you are discovering, experiencing, and wondering.

If you engage with the Living Word, you can confidently expect to know God's love for you and for everyone. As His presence comes to you it will show through you as evidence of His ongoing creative work in His unshakeable kingdom, as you Live Wide Awake.

No one learns the same. No one relates the same. We have varying interests and experiences with reading the Bible. Be honest: what do you think about it? Is it boring? Is it over your head? What is your history with reading it? What do you want from it? What do you hope will happen when you open it?

I have come to consider the Bible as less of a book and more as the active, relevant, life-giving, and necessary Living Word. From here on I will be using those words. You're welcome to join me. Changing my language has changed my heart.

This book deserves more than your drive-by time. It is intended for sitting down and drawing near. These devotions will take you into the deep places of an inexhaustible, unchanging, unconditional Love. You'll want time to soak that in.

I offer you some of my stories to wake up yours. The stories are followed by a variety of Pay-Attention Practices for you to engage with the Living Word. Please try them all, even if they are unfamiliar or make you uncomfortable. If you do engage, I promise you will find ways that make the Word come alive. I know you are going to be delighted when words come off the page, truth hits home, and the voice of God speaks specifically to you. Let the practices take your hand and lead you nearer to the Father's good heart.

Following each chapter there is a call to let the Word walk--to confidently share your own story and God's story in your own words and actions with at least one person. Have fun doing it! If you have extra time or desire to keep digging in, there is an option to Go Deeper.

"When you know perfect Love and the expert Lover of you, it's impossible not to tell someone. It's impossible not to be changed."

The Caffeinated Woman

My desire is to be a thoughtful voice with a fresh and honest approach to spiritual formation. Though I'm not an expert, I am a lifetime disciple of Jesus. I offer you these stories and invite you to see yourself in His story. Be compelled to love who you are and know who God is, that you might Live Wide Awake.

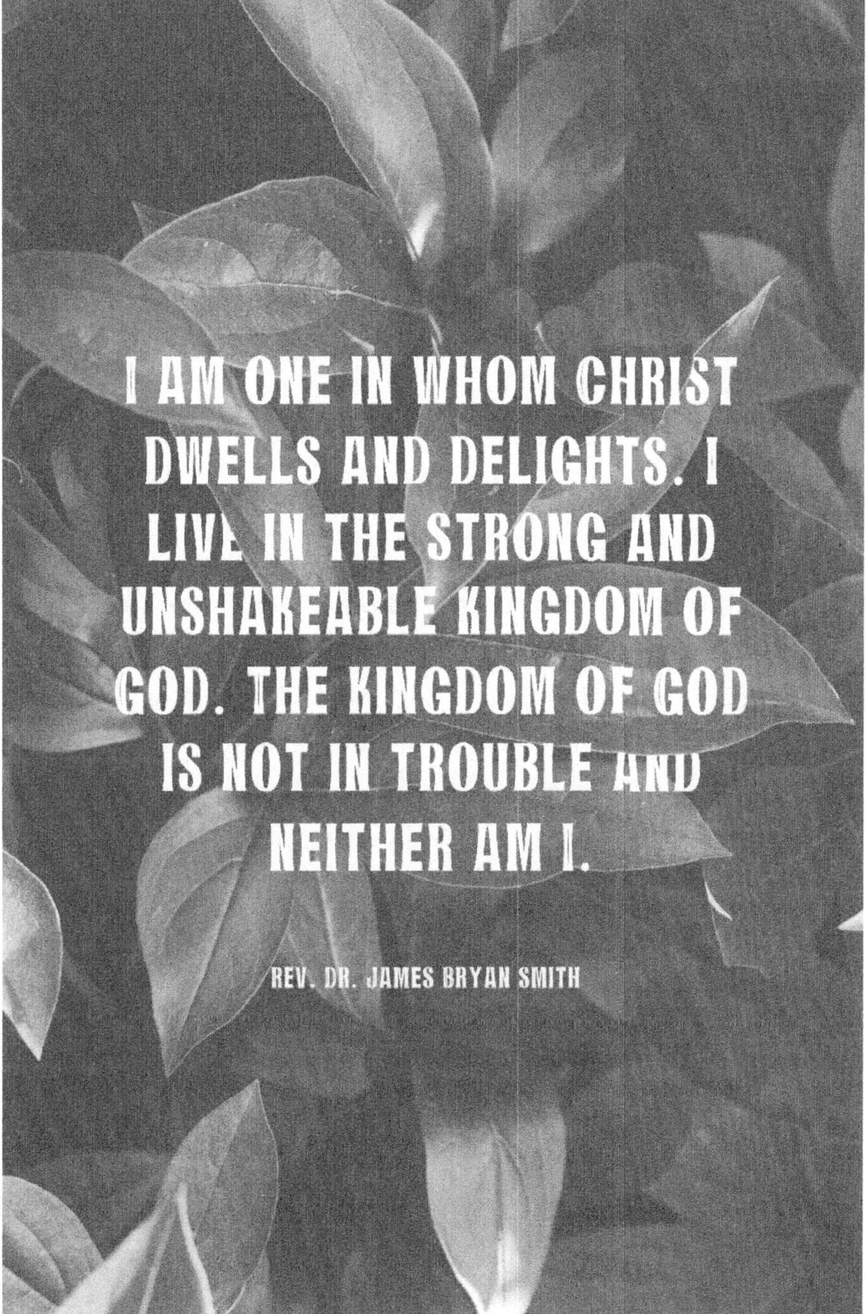
I AM ONE IN WHOM CHRIST DWELLS AND DELIGHTS. I LIVE IN THE STRONG AND UNSHAKEABLE KINGDOM OF GOD. THE KINGDOM OF GOD IS NOT IN TROUBLE AND NEITHER AM I.
REV. DR. JAMES BRYAN SMITH

Wildflowers and Roses

My sister Julia had a peculiar talent for choosing the perfect card for anyone, no matter the occasion. I've realized in hindsight she was an encourager. Maybe she found in cards the right thing to say that she couldn't say herself. She loved to read cards and always laughed out loud, even snorting if the card was funny enough, which would in turn make me laugh out loud too. When I turned 40, my mother sent me the perfect card. She must have learned from Julia.

I was "a strong-willed child." I didn't choose to be that way, it's just how I showed up in the world. According to the experts, strong-willed children thrive if parents and other significant adults guide their will toward desired choices and actions. Shutting down, controlling, or crushing their will doesn't have healthy outcomes. Thankfully, I had enough people who did their best to steer, corral, and encourage me when I was young. I've learned and am still learning to direct my will toward obedience, patience, and peace.

Here's what my mother's card said:

> *"Before I knew I'd been given a wildflower to love instead of a rose, I'd wonder to myself...'How will I ever calm this girl down enough to get her to adulthood?'*
>
> *"You bounded & jumped & shimmered & swayed through the hills of childhood. Needless to say, we didn't always see eye to eye as I tried to peer around corners for you so you wouldn't get hurt...*

> *"You still amaze me with all of your colors & ideas & energy. It's so incredible to be given a child who helps you plant your flowers outside of the garden.*
>
> *Love you, my Wild Flower Girl!"*

My mom was and still is one of the most influential people in my life. If I had to describe her as a flower, she is a Rose. She is organized, efficient, and hospitable. She is a natural caregiver and is highly skilled in the kitchen, behind a sewing machine, and with a pen and notecard. Her life is full of people. She serves them, enjoys them, helps them, makes time for them, and listens to them. Most importantly, she prays for them. Her knees are calloused. Her heart is humble. Her soul is wise. She loves her Father deeply. She wanted ten children and had five. I was number one. Apparently my strong-willed nature influenced that number.

It's easy to define ourselves by what people have said about us, or by our personalities, or what we do for a living, or what we are good at or notorious for. What will transform us, though, is the truth about the God of love--the truth of being made, known, loved, and constantly cared for by the Almighty. It is life-changing. Let these be the messages that define who you are.

Pay Attention Practice One

I am a speed reader. I can inhale a book. It's easy to rush through reading the Bible. It is not as easy to do so if you approach the Living Word as if it has something important to tell you, about you.

I spent a month reading this Psalm daily. I am going to encourage you to do it for a week. Think of it as a perfect card God chose for you.

Psalm 139
For the choir director: A psalm of David.

> O Lord, you have examined my heart and know everything about me.
>
> You know when I sit down or stand up.
>
> You know my thoughts even when I'm far away. You see me when I travel and when I rest at home.
>
> You know everything I do.
>
> You know what I am going to say even before I say it, Lord.
>
> You go before me and follow me.
>
> You place your hand of blessing on my head.
>
> Such knowledge is too wonderful for me, too great for me to understand!
>
> I can never escape from your Spirit! I can never get away from your presence!

If I go up to heaven, you are there; if I go down to the grave, you are there.

If I ride the wings of the morning, if I dwell by the farthest oceans, even there your hand will guide me, and your strength will support me.

I could ask the darkness to hide me and the light around me to become night—but even in darkness I cannot hide from you.

To you the night shines as bright as day. Darkness and light are the same to you.

You made all the delicate, inner parts of my body and knit me together in my mother's womb.

Thank you for making me so wonderfully complex! Your workmanship is marvelous—how well I know it.

You watched me as I was being formed in utter seclusion, as I was woven together in the dark of the womb.

You saw me before I was born. Every day of my life was recorded in your book.

Every moment was laid out before a single day had passed.

How precious are your thoughts about me, O God. They cannot be numbered!

I can't even count them; they outnumber the grains of sand!

And when I wake up, you are still with me!

O God, if only you would destroy the wicked!

> Get out of my life, you murderers!
>
> They blaspheme you; your enemies misuse your name.
>
> O Lord, shouldn't I hate those who hate you?
>
> Shouldn't I despise those who oppose you. Yes, I hate them with total hatred, for your enemies are my enemies.
>
> Search me, O God, and know my heart; test me and know my anxious thoughts.
>
> Point out anything in me that offends you, and lead me along the path of everlasting life.[3]

Highlight, underline, circle, or draw arrows pointing at what is true about God.

Read Psalm 139 again slowly.

Choose phrases or words that speak the truth about who you are and write them down.

Example: I am someone who can never get away from the Presence of God.

Read the psalm again, slowly. Choose phrases or verses that stand out to you about who God is. Each day repeat them out loud, or hand letter them, write them on your mirror, or put them on a reminder on your phone.

Pay Attention Practice Two

Read Psalm 139 verses 1-6.
God knows you. He knows everything.

Imagine meeting Jesus one-on-one. He says, "Tell me about yourself." Put a chair across from where you are sitting. Answer Jesus' question out loud, directing your words towards the chair where he would be sitting.

Read verses 1-6 again.
What is it like for you to speak directly, out loud to Jesus? How do you feel about being completely known by God?

Pay Attention Practice Three

God is with you. Always. It's easier to believe when all is well, but God is with us even when things are chaotic.

My hubby JR and I moved from Colorado to south Florida where we had no contacts. Verse nine became a source of hope I clung to. I needed that guidance, strength, and support of the Spirit of God. Often I wondered if we had made a mistake by leaving Colorado, if we were disobedient. Every time those thoughts popped in my mind, this question would follow:

"Why do you think you've made a mistake? Why do you think you didn't follow the leading of the Lord to Florida?"

I thought about that a few times, but eventually I realized the answer was always the same. "It's really hard here."

Does ongoing, long-term struggle make you question the place you find yourself? Does adversity make you question God? Those circumstances might. It's natural for humans to avoid what is hard and want to fix what is wrong. We want pain and suffering to cease quickly. Yet, sometimes we must stay in the rough places. Sometimes suffering lasts a long time. It is true, what stated in these verses: who is with us matters most. Who we rely on for support and strength even if there isn't a quick resolve matters most. Believing God, even through the suffering, matters most.

What is going on in this season of life? Write down what you have to accomplish, what is difficult, or what is delightful. Is there any new thought in these verses that would make a difference when you look back at what you wrote down? Talk to God about that.

Note: If the concept of "talking to God" is something new or unusual to you, try this. Imagine you are in a car, Jesus is in the driver's seat, and you are in the passenger seat. You are on a road trip and Jesus knows the destination; He is focused on the road. You have plenty of time, no distractions, and Jesus is all ears. Now start talking.

Read Psalm 139: 7-12.
David, the author of the Psalm, uses comparison, metaphor, hyperbole, and other figures of speech in this poetic song (I am certain he never literally rode morning's wings). Pay attention to each description of what man might try to do and what God would do. Write out a personal interpretation of David's figurative language.

Pay Attention Practice Four

My husband and I have friends who are young adults, young married couples, or young parents. It is so much fun to know them and later get to share in knowing their children. We fawn over the babies. It is easy to look at a baby and only see a precious, adorable gift. However, I dare say that is rarely how we look at our grown selves. Before you read these verses, stand in front of a mirror and look at yourself. Pay attention to what you think when you look at your reflection. Read the Living Word out loud so you can hear the words as if Jesus is saying them to His precious child.

Read Psalm 139: 13-16
Write down what stands out to you.

Pay Attention Practice Five

Recite this prayer before your time with Jesus today:

"I consent to the presence of God with me, His words to me, His love for me. I will remain in His presence with love today."

Read Psalm 139
Sit with your eyes closed and use your imagination to observe Jesus as He walks into a room where you are sitting on a wide windowsill, waiting to spend time together. You get a chance to be face to face.

What words come to mind to describe his demeanor as he walks toward you?
How is he dressed?
What does his face look like when He looks directly at you?
Does He say anything?
How do you act when Jesus approaches you?
How do you feel?
What are you thinking?
Do you say anything?
What would you like to do together?

Take a minute and write down any images you saw, words you heard, questions you had, or emotions that came up.

Let's use David's poetic language to remember always that God made and knows His children, both as is and as they will be. We love who we are by listening and responding to our Father.

Use verses 17-18 and 23-24 as prayer.

NOTE: Verses 19-22 used to stump me. After some study I came to understand them as David talking to God about the offensive things his enemies had done toward God. He follows that by asking God to take inventory of his heart and point out things he had done that were offensive to God.

The heart is the will, the control center of human beings. It is where our emotions, motivations, thoughts, and actions live and flow from.

After soaking up this Psalm, consider: who is God to you? How does he define your importance?

Let The Word Walk

I have not yet met anyone who doesn't need Good News. Let us pay attention to what Jesus is doing in our own lives, to where we see God. Then, let's tell someone else about what we are seeing, hearing, and learning. We can know that God is with us, still loving the world he created. For the next two days, look for an opportunity to share with at least one person, either in writing or in person, at least one thing about what you discovered from this Psalm about God or about those whom he made wonderfully complex.

Go Deeper

Turn to the artwork at the beginning of this section of the book. Read each sentence and write a personal response to it.

Repeat it daily and pay attention to how it impacts your heart and mind.

If there are words or concepts you would like to dig into deeper, use a concordance or dictionary to look up meanings, scripture references, historical significance, and definitions.

Big Girl Pants

I am about to tell you a very embarrassing story.

I spent a lot of years being profoundly and perpetually tired. Every parent of young children knows what it's like to function while tired. It's not sustainable, but it is doable. This kind of tiredness happened long after my children were grown up.

Living perpetually and profoundly tired has long-term negative side effects on the heart. When I mentioned the tiredness to my mom, she said, "Well, we are just sleepy people. You've always been a good napper."

That's fine if you're two, but it is not great if you're 52...and I'm past 52.

I mentioned this profound and perpetual tiredness to my nurse practitioner, Natasha Peoples. I followed that by insisting I sleep well. She stifled a laugh then gently suggested a sleep study. I pictured lying in bed in a room with a one-sided window, while the people sitting behind it watched me sleep. The thought of strangers listening to me snore was appalling. Sleep study huh? No, I thought, I'm not doing that.

Natasha informed me a sleep doctor would send me home with a device to wear in my own bed. It would measure my heart and breathing, then the doctors would review the data and tell me the results. In the moment, she was convincing. I agreed.

A few weeks later, the sleep study people called me to set up an appointment, I said: “Well, you know, I’m fine. Never mind.”

I totally chickened out.

I continued to be profoundly and perpetually tired. Many months passed. My husband often transferred to the couch, and I hated sleeping apart. I sent my Nurse Practitioner an email and confessed to chickening out. I wrote, “I am ready to pull my big girl pajama pants up over my chicken legs and get that sleep study done.”

The second call from the sleep study people resulted in an appointment. I showed up to the sleep study office very nervous. I talked way too fast and said ridiculous things to a baby-faced sleep study doctor, who luckily had a good enough sense of humor to say back to me: “It sounds like you’re ready to pull your big girl pajama pants up over your chicken legs and get this sleep study done.”

I was speechless. My confession had traveled.

I did the study at home. Three weeks later I got the diagnosis: I had “moderate” sleep apnea, just a number or two under “severe.” I couldn’t believe it. I mistakenly thought apnea was related to old age, disease, or weight. Turns out, none of that is true and it is much more common than you might think. I now have a nighttime oxygen-dispensing machine, called the c-pap. It came with flowers on it. The flowers don’t help.

I have a love-HATE relationship with the machine. In the first three weeks, I only hated it. Then I started noticing a difference. Now, I notice a giant difference. Breathing oxygen all night makes me feel refreshed the next day. I am no longer profoundly and perpetually tired. I love how I feel.

However, I hate how the embarrassing mask I have to wear in front of my husband makes me look. I've told him that if he ever laughs at me, he has to take me to a very expensive dinner of my choice. It's most motivating for an accountant. So far, no fancy meal.

I am still embarrassed by this diagnosis--but I am sharing something I would prefer to keep private because it's a powerful example of evidence on the surface of my life that was telling me something needed attention under the surface. When I denied the problem, I stayed physically unhealthy. When I finally accepted there was a problem, I engaged in the solution. This is belief and behavior coming together toward healing.

All of us will find evidence on the outside of our life that points to something inside that needs attention. The evidence might appear as fearfulness, defensiveness, criticalness, bitterness, greediness, selfishness, or (as in my case) sleepiness. These are signs we need to look at and lean into for our hearts to be healed and whole.

First I want to grant you permission to acknowledge you are fragile sometimes. It's alright. It's very human of you. Be gentle with yourself. Other people are sometimes fragile, too. They are also human.

Second, I invite you to look at what is trying to get your attention. When you see symptoms of unhealthy behavior, be honest and name it. This is an exercise in awareness, acceptance, and healing. This is not and I repeat NOT an exercise in judgment or shame. This work leads broken people toward wholeness.

There are Holy mentors--meet with them. There are helpful healers--listen to them. There is a Holy Living Word--engage with it. You belong to a Holy God--pay attention to Him. Our duty as Holy people is to cooperate, not collide, with God who loves us extravagantly.

Fellow follower of Jesus, love yourself well, and let's get to the business of Living Wide Awake.

Pay Attention Practice One

I once asked a young friend of mine to tell me about her relationship with God. She proceeded to share real and raw information, though nearly every sentence included the word 'church.' When she was done I thanked her for telling me all about her relationship to the church. She had not mentioned God. I took my palms face up and laid one on each of her shoulders. I moved my hands together up and over her head, as if I was lifting something heavy. I explained I was removing the mantle of the church off her shoulders and was going to set it right next to her. She could have it back later.

I asked again, "Now, tell me about your relationship with God."

She cried and replied, "I'm not sure what to say."

Though the following questions might generate some strong defensive feelings when you read them, or maybe even guilty feelings, that isn't why I included them. These are questions meant to dissect our relationships to God and with the church you attend. It will help us see how they are different and how they are connected.

Ephesians 1
This book is a letter from Paul to believers. Read Ephesians 1: 1-2

Do you identify with any of these descriptions: "saint," "holy person," or "faithful follower?"

Do you consider yourself more of a church follower or a Jesus follower?

What motivates you to carve out time for church? What motivates you to make space to be one-on-one with Jesus?

What keeps you away from church or one-on-one time with Jesus?

If you and I were on my front porch and I asked you to tell me about your relationship to God, without using the word "church," what would you highlight? Who is God to you, and who are you to Him? What are your bullet points? What story would you tell me? Write out your answer, and read it over to yourself.

Read Ephesians 1:3-5
The relationship between you and God is specific. What does the Living Word say about God? About Jesus?

Do you live as if this is true?

What does it say about who you are? Can you learn to love that about yourself?

Pay Attention Practice Two

Draw three large circles on a piece of paper. Put the name God the Father in one, Jesus the Son in another, and the Holy Spirit in the final one.

Read or listen to Ephesians 1: 3-14. It is one long sentence with an emphasis on praise. Write down the activity and blessings of Father God, Jesus, and the Holy Spirit in their circle. Do you see how the Father, Son, and Spirit work together as one? Is there anything you find amazing? Is there something you've never understood before?

Do you see yourself living from a posture of someone who is the child of an abundantly generous God?

Is there any evidence on the outside of your life that indicates something underneath doesn't believe you're blessed, forgiven, or the focus of God's love?

Name at least one thing that gives you a reason to love who you are.

Finish your time today praising the Father, Son, and Spirit.

> *It is in Christ that we find out who we are and what we are living for. Ephesians 1: 11 the Message*

Pay Attention Practice Three

We present ourselves to the world via our personality. Beneath the personality is our essence: who we are at our core, our true self, our identity. Identity is defined as the condition of being oneself and not another. Identity comes with issues when our personality attaches itself to descriptors that are not true or are incomplete. Struggles with identity come from deciding which voices speak the truth. Our true identity comes from the author of our life.

There are many truths about our identity in this passage, and you need to know them. They will help you untangle half-truths and outright lies you've believed. They will set your feet, your mind, and your tender heart on what is remarkable and solid.

Eph 1: 3-14
Print out these verses on a separate piece of paper or write them out by hand.

Circle every "we," "us," "our," and "you." Underline what is said about we/us/our/you. List the truths about who you are from this passage. Make it personal, using "I" or "me."

Example: God loved me and chose me to be Holy and whole before He created the world. He has always loved me.

If we live as if these statements are true, we love who we are. Loving who we are is based on our identity with Jesus Christ, and this translates into our ability to love others. This is a healthy, holy love we are blessed to receive and release.

Pay Attention Practice Four

Read Ephesians 1: 15-23

Do you want to know God? Paul prayed that request constantly for his faithful followers. I had not prayed for that for myself or for others until I started soaking up this chapter.

I borrowed the words from Ephesians 1: 17-18 from The Message to create a prayer of love for ourselves and others. Pray this prayer by inserting pronouns for yourself (me, I) and the names of people who come to mind. Pray it continually.

God, of our Master Jesus, will you make ____ intelligent and discerning in knowing you personally, intimately. Make the eyes of ____ (my, their) heart focused and clear so ____ (I/they) can see exactly what it is You are calling ___ to do. Let ____ grasp the immensity of this glorious way of life You have for ____, for all your followers. Oh, the utter extravagance of Your work in ____, in all of us who trust You, endless energy, boundless strength. Let ____ behavior reflect ____ belief. Heal the places where that is broken.

Pay Attention Practice Five

Read Ephesians 1: 19-23

We learn to love who we are when we know the God of love, because our identity and purpose comes from Him.

Take each verse by itself and write down one thing you wonder about God and one thing you know about God.

Take each verse and write down what is said about you, about others, and about creation.

If you believe all this to be true, how could it change your interactions with creation? How could it affect your interactions with everyone you come into contact with?

I don't believe we can fully understand the mysteries of God, the greatness of His power, the spiritual blessings lavished on us, or how Jesus Christ fills all things everywhere. But I do so love pondering these things in my heart. I hope you do too.

Set a timer for five minutes and ponder these questions. Pay attention to what comes to mind, or what feelings arise.

What if **Christ** is everywhere?
What **if** Christ is everywhere?
What if Christ is everywhere?
What if Christ is **everywhere?**

"I would say that my only real definition of a Christian is one who can see Christ everywhere else and even in oneself."

Richard Rohr[4]

Let The Word Walk

Our belief and behavior need to be reconciled regarding our relationship to God, to ourselves, and to others. Paul talked to the people in Ephesus about how Jesus is always working to bring everything and everyone together. He shares the good news that we get to participate in this work of reconciliation. We have work to do in our own heart, leaning into an honest evaluation of our opinions, attitudes, reactions, and responses to people, places, and things in our lives.

As a way to let the Word walk this week, write a raw, honest letter to God, confidently presenting what might be broken. Discuss your harmful opinions, attitudes, actions, and words as an act of surrender, an ask for help and healing.

What a wonderful way to love who you are.

Going Deeper

There might have been words, phrases, or concepts in this chapter that are hard to understand. Take the time to look up those words in a Bible dictionary or commentary until they make sense to you, instead of letting them stay confusing. Or, start a conversation with your pastor, a Bible study teacher, or another wise person whom you believe to be spiritually mature.

Know Who You're Not

When I was in high school I had a best friend named Amy. Her mom used to say that if Amy and I were not friends, "Laura wouldn't get any school work done and Amy wouldn't have any fun." Amy was the class president; I was the class clown. She was the team captain; I provided camaraderie.

I always wanted to be an identical twin, exactly like another person. Though completely impossible, there was a day on a senior class trip, when Amy and I wore matching shirts with 3/4 length sleeves and a rainbow on the front. We both french braided our long blonde hair. We wore bell bottom jeans and the same blue tennis shoes. We spent every moment together riding roller coasters and eating junk food. The highlight of that day for me though, was all the people who asked if we were twins.

Funny enough, I now have twin girls--though they're fraternal. What I know now is that twins are completely separate people. My girls liked a lot of the same foods, activities, sports, subjects, and people growing up, but interacted with them uniquely. My husband and I rarely called them "the twins." We referred to them by their names, or "the girls," or, quite often, "Thing One and Thing Two." Those nicknames are still effective when trying to get their attention.

Striving to be like someone else is a significant contributor to anxiety. Trying to get others to change, act like we want them to act, work according to our standards, or make choices we think are the best also adds anxiety. Casual entertainment on Facebook, Instagram, and other social media have created a platform of comparison leading to serious discontentment with who we are, what we look like, where we've been, and what we have. People-pleasing continues to be a behavior that leads to living anxiously. It's a losing game. I see it. I've done it. I hate it.

Though we may not acknowledge it, we create anxiety by trying to fix people so they can think politically, relationally, religiously, socially, economically, or practically the way *we* do. We are *not* people fixers. You *cannot* change someone else. If you are heavily invested in this industry, my best advice is to Fire Yourself.

In this chapter, I grant you permission to know who you are NOT:

You are not made in the image of Instagram. You are not Queen of Everything. You are not always right. You are not someone else. You are not finished yet. You are not too much. And the "I'm not enough" voice needs to shut-up.

There is no other person on Earth like you, and there never will be. Amen.

The first time I took a personality profile test, I had an epiphany. There were words to describe how I was wired. There was an explanation for the way I interacted with the world. I heard reasons for my strengths and my struggles. I found language to describe what made me tick, what motivated me, what environments I would thrive in. This information was profound and transformed me from viewing my impulsive nature and ability to talk to anyone anywhere as an embarrassing problem that needed fixing, to seeing myself as an energizing presence. I was a child who so often heard "be quiet," "slow down," "you talk too much," "you are too much," and "you do too much." The personality assessment reframed my natural way of being into something positive, and showed me where the world needed those character traits.

I began to understand who I was not. I identified I would always naturally struggle with details, organization, and time management. A job sitting at a desk for eight hours would never be a good fit. The more awareness I had of myself, who I was, and who I was not, relieved me from the anxiety of trying to be all things to all people in all places. The relief led to realistic expectations and acceptance.

The ongoing work of self-awareness and acceptance has helped me be able to observe others through the lense of curiosity, noting their strengths and their natural ways of being and doing. As I surrender my need to fix or change other people, I am learning to accept them for who they are, and who they are not. This too is a relief.

Acceptance, according to John Ortberg, is defined as "a remarkable action, difficult to define, yet unmistakable when we experience it. To accept people is to be for them. It is to recognize that it is a very good thing that these people are alive and to long for the best for them. It does not mean to approve of everything they do. It means to want what is best for their soul no matter what they do."[5]

Do you know what happens when you learn about yourself, when you practice self-awareness, when you accept who you are and who you're not? Three significant shifts in perspective:

1. You begin to love the true version of yourself.
2. You become aware and accepting of who others are.

3. You love God for making you just the way He designed you. Eventually, you learn to see others as humans God made just as fearfully and wonderfully.

When you shift your behavior because you've shifted your perspective:

1. You can love God with everything you've got.
2. You can love other humans as God loves them.
3. You can love yourself as God loves you--and that kind of love works its way into your life.
4. People-pleasing loses its attraction. People-fixing has less appeal. We may not love this way perfectly, but Jesus said it was the most important way to live. He makes it possible.

The shift in behavior led me away from wanting to be exactly like someone else. It will lead you to acknowledging you want to be the best version of *yourself.* Awareness and acceptance lead to addressing wounds and broken behavior. You find language to describe your true-self which helps you knock down insecurities and stand confidently in your own skin. You discover that loving yourself is how you're able to love others naturally and sacrificially. You are on the road to being healed and whole and Holy. You will invite others to join you on this road.

To know who you're not is a giant relief.

Pay Attention Practice One

You Are Not Finished Yet.

When I read that statement, I can't help but hear Paul telling the people in Philippi he was confident, "that God, who began a good work in you, will continue his work until it is finally finished on the day when Christ Jesus returns." (Philippians 1:6) We are not finished, but we will be! The kingdom of God is already present, but not yet complete. We are part of that kingdom.

(Revisit the art work at the beginning of this section of the book.)

Read or listen to Philippians 1.
Underline the words Good News.

We need to be able to spread the good news, because there is a world full of people who need it. I've found believers are afraid to do so because they think they need to be able to explain anything the Bible says. That is not true.

Write out the good news about Jesus, who He is, what He's done, and what He means to you. Record how your life is different because of your relationship to Jesus in your own words, your own story of faith. This might be the most important work you do in the work of loving who you are and knowing who God is so you can live wide awake.

Pay Attention Practice Two

You are Not Superhuman.

Once upon a time, I lived at mach speed with my hair on fire, burning the candle at both ends. I gave 110 percent for all the things I said yes to: making calls, coordinating people, showing up to meetings, working events, cleaning up afterward, checking in with people, cheerleading the group to the finish line. Then I would crash, burn, unravel, swear, cry, eat a container of ice cream, and resent the people who took too much from me.

One day my husband pointed out the pattern, called it unhealthy, and suggested something needed to change. He said that in love, and it helped me stare that junk in the face and own it.

Acknowledging unhealthy behavior is uncomfortable. It is easier for us to deny it, defend it, and let it go on. A few trustworthy people helped me unpack why I was living that life cycle. I had to address issues of insecurity, uncertainty, and pride. Then I got to learn different ways to care for myself, which began with this admission: I am not the queen of everything.

Once, on a vacation by the sea, God and I had a good conversation. I walked out into the ocean waves and told my Superwoman persona she had to go. I thanked her for the good times and valuable lessons, then sent her off to swim far, far away.

My personality will always tend toward that, but the essence of my inner being does not require any of it. I don't want that anymore. I want to keep choosing healthy over superhuman.

According to Tony Schwartz, one of the leading voices for (human) energy-management,

"Between digital technology and rising complexity, there's more information and more requests coming at us, faster and more relentlessly than ever. Unlike computers, however, human beings aren't meant to operate continuously, at high speeds, for long periods of time. Rather, we're designed to move rhythmically between high and low electrical frequencies. Our hearts beat at varying intervals. Our lungs expand and contract depending on demand. It's not sufficient to be good at inhaling. Indeed, the more deeply you exhale, the calmer and more capable you become."[6]

Before you engage with the Living Word today, practice this breathing exercise as prayer of being present. Sit comfortably in a chair, hands open on your lap. Notice how your body feels. Pay attention to where you might be holding tension, or how your mind is racing. Take in a deep breath and hold it for three seconds. Slowly exhale. Relax. Do this three times.

Notice how your body feels now. Usually this practice will release some tension and slow down the thoughts so you can focus.

Read Philippians 2: 1-18 slowly.
Write out verses 5-8. What words seem surprising for the Son of God?

Read 1-18 again, listening for what would help you if you struggle with accepting you're not queen or king of everything. If you sense a personal word for your superhuman self, write it on a piece of paper you can keep in your pocket. Look at it multiple times this week.

Pay Attention Practice Three

You are Not a Human "Doing."

Most of the time I am just trying to do the best I can. My best has triumphs and tricky spots, sacred moments and roller coaster rides. Honestly, I spend a lot of thought, time, energy, and effort on what I do. When I listen to someone share about their busy lives, the overwhelming pile of things to accomplish, or the unsustainable pace they're moving at, it's easy to remind them they are a human *being*, not a human *doing*.

It's not as easy to hear those words and apply them to myself.

You can love who you are by paying attention to your being and what Jesus is doing for you.

Read Philippians 3 - 4:1 as if Paul was your close friend who came over to share his story. He wants to encourage you, a fellow friend of Jesus. His focus is on Jesus's doing and our being.

Write a list of questions you want to ask Paul.

What is the main point Paul got across to you? Write it out in your own words.

Pay Attention Practice Four

You Are Not Always Right.

> *"What's true about people wherever you go is they like to be comfortable with what they know."*
>
> **The Caffeinated Woman**

When my father was in his last months of life, we paid very close attention to his wisdom, advice, opinions, and viewpoints. I didn't agree with them all, but I did have great respect for my father. When a person is facing their final days, what they use their energy to say is worth taking note of.

"You are not always right."

I heard my dad say this over and over in his last few months. He said it to his children, his friends, and family. That statement was profound, coming from a man who usually spoke with authority and pride as if he *were* right all the time. I wondered if this came from a new place of humility, and sharing this new wisdom with others was his way of apologizing.

Having worked in Hospice, I learned about and saw thin spaces people live in when they are at the end of this temporary life. The distance between earthly life and divine life is close. Some take care of unfinished business that has been neglected for years. Some tell buried stories no one knew were there. Some make peace with their demons and their enemies and themselves. Many have conversations with loved ones who have already gone from this temporary life. Some speak profound truth from a pure heart.

God is the only one who is always right. We may be right on occasion, just not all the time. Living from a posture of knowing it all and being the authority on what's right can be a signpost of fear, insecurity, defensiveness, deception, or deep and unhealed wounds. Thinking we are always right is a sign of being human. Accepting you are not always right is a sign of wisdom.

If you react to reading this, pay attention to your reaction.

Can you identify a sense of right that you feel the need to defend? Does it hold you hostage? Do you hold other people hostage with it? If so, let's take it to Jesus, who is slow to anger, full of mercy, and interested in your freedom.

Read Philippians Chapter 4: 2-9 slowly.

Paul addresses two specific women who knew the Good News and worked hard with Paul. He cared enough to call them and their conflict out by name.

Read it out loud. Listen for words that stand out.

Reread quietly. Listen to where words connect with your life. Talk to God about what seems highlighted. Journal or speak out loud.

Read it one last time. Rest quietly in the Presence and love of God. Thank Him as you finish your time together.

Let the Word Walk

Share with someone you trust your insights about who you are not and what you've learned through meditating on Philippians.
Or
Ask God for the opportunity to encourage someone with the Good News of what Jesus has done and is doing for them.

Go deeper

Do some reflecting on your being and your doing. This reflection is healthy self-awareness, which requires paying attention to the present condition of your inner environment.

Draw a large circle in the center of a sheet of paper. Inside the circle, write down what you are like when you are functioning out of your best, healthiest, well-rested, confident, and content self. Draw a square around the circle. Inside the square write down what you are like when you are stressed, overwhelmed, or at the end of your rope.

Around the square write down all of the things that you do, that you feel responsible for, and that you think you need to have control over.

Can you make connections between your doing and your being, your best and being stressed? Draw lines to connect.

Is there something that needs attention, help, healing, processing, forgiving, or letting go? If so, what action can you take to address the needs of your inner environment?

"To choose growth is noble. To actually grow is messier than a pigpen. Extend grace to yourself."

Mike Kim[7]

TELL ME ABOUT YOURSELF

"The actual thing you want to do forever is be you,"

Annie F. Downs to Emily P. Freeman[8]

Who are you?

If you introduced yourself to me, what would you say? If your mom introduced you, what would she say? If your professor, pastor, neighbor or employer introduced you, how would they describe you to me? If your spouse or best friend was giving an introduction, what do you think they would highlight about you?

When my mom describes me, she brings up having read the *Strong-Willed Child* before I was four. She remembers my constant movement, my large cache of friends, and confidence. She would tell you I was a very happy and determined little girl. And as a teenager, I was strongly opinionated about injustices in my life, more invested in extracurriculars than academics, and forthcoming about what I was thinking, feeling and doing often to the detriment of her sleep at night. Post high school she would mention a season of unsettlement and reticence to share much. And now, she would say "passionate" dominates the way I love food, family, people, and Jesus. She would highlight how I care about spiritual matters, entertaining, and meaningful, healthy relationships. She may have included the term "overextended," too, but I am battling that down more often than letting it win.

What do you think Jesus would say if I asked him to tell me about you?

An important note here. If you ponder that question and shaming, hurtful, or untrue statements come to mind, those words are not of the Lord. Reject those words. Listen again for the good and merciful voice of your Creator.

One evening, I was invited to a girls' night with a group of women from our apartment complex. We had dinner at The Living Room, a restaurant with an eclectic atmosphere and a creative menu. That evening there was live music by local musicians and a tarot card reader available for free. Everyone at my table (except me) met with her individually. All returned crying. Initially, I was baffled by their identically strong responses. Then I listened. I later concluded every one of them needed a dose of hope, and thought they found it in this woman who told them about their life, both present and future as if she knew them. As good-hearted as she might have been, this woman was a stranger. Whatever information she shared wasn't based in truth, love, or intimacy.

The greatest human need is to know and be known and to love and be loved. Those who know and love us well, truly, and deeply are good sources of hope, but human knowing and loving are limited and imperfect, even at their best. What is true is known perfectly only by God. Listen to what Jesus said to people he knew and loved:

> *"I am the good shepherd; I know my sheep and my sheep know me--just as the Father knows me and I know the Father—and I lay down my life for the sheep" (John 10:14-15).*

Those are the words of truth, love, intimacy.

We spend an exhausting amount of time and energy being concerned about what other people think of us. What we think people are thinking can strongly influence what we do. Our conclusions are followed by actions aimed at making those people approve of us. It's common and understandable when the love of people matters more to us than the unconditional love of God.

To live wide awake is to let the thoughts of God about you matter most. Living wide awake by loving who you are is a result of becoming more and more aware of how God knows and loves you. An ongoing transformation then happens in your inner being and permeates your attitudes and actions.

Today, let the extravagant love of God in. Let it matter most. Let it sink deep so you might know God and fall in love with Him. Listen closely and understand who you are. Then you will know the hope God has for you--reliable concrete, unchangeable hope.

Pay Attention Practice One

You are created Imago Dei, in the image of God.

My daughters, Lauren and Lyndsay, are both nurses. They care for people in the emergency room and the ICU, meeting a slice of all of humanity in urgent and frightening places. In their nurse training, they were taught not only how to care for people medically, but how to see every patient first as an image-bearer of God, no matter who they are. Lyndsay shared these thoughts:

"Working as a nurse has shown me that we all share a common thread of humanity. We are a broken, sinful people, yet we all bear the image of God. I realized how I automatically put myself in the middle of my universe, fixing my eyes on my wants and needs. Caring for patients and families through illness reoriented my gaze toward Christ. There, I was continually reminded life is a gift. Each person has a story within God's story of sacrifice, love, grace, and redemption. We must look into the eyes of everyone as best as we are able and practice empathy, compassion, and humility by listening to one another's stories and respecting each person as God's image-bearer."

Lauren shared these thoughts:

"Working in the emergency room is a microcosm of the messiness of life. Nurses love to try to fix people. As a nurse, I want to solve their problems, give them their discharge papers with a bow on them, and have them walk out the hospital door feeling healed and whole. In my senior year of nursing school in a community rotation working with a homeless population, my professor gently reminded me that 'people don't necessarily want your life.' Though startling, the truth of that statement changed my perspective.

One of my favorite authors, Emily P. Freeman, speaks to how a changed perspective began to change me:"

"The earlier question, how can I help [them]? is changing into a new question; how can I see [them]? How will Immanuel show himself right now, not just for [them] in [their] pain but for me in my self-obsession? God with us is big enough to handle us both. When I release my obsession with finding a cure, I can embrace the desire to be curious. This person, this friend, is not a project or an assignment. [They are] an image-bearer...when people are hurting, searching, and in difficult places, they don't want my bag filled with skills. They don't want me to rush to solutions. They simply want me as I am, where I am, fully alive"[9]

Dear Image Bearer of God,
Who are you? Write down a top 20 list of what it's like to be you.

Dear Image Bearer of God,
You zoomed in on yourself for a few minutes, now zoom out and think about yourself as part of all humans created in the image of God. This is how God's story begins. If the passages about God creating people are familiar to you, I am inviting you to read with curiosity. Approach the reading by releasing what you may already know to let yourself wonder. Read through the passages slowly and write out as many questions as your curiosity brings up. Start your sentences with, "I wonder." Here is an example:

I wonder why men and women were made at separate times?

Genesis 1: 26-31
Genesis 2:18-25

Who are you according to your Creator?

Pay Attention Practice Two

You are gifted uniquely.

There are several resources available to help people understand how they are naturally inclined to view and interact with the world. Some of my personal favorites are StrengthsFinder, The Enneagram, DISC, and The Call. At the point in time, I took my first personality assessment, I would honestly say my self-awareness was minuscule. Upon reading the results, my jaw dropped, my eyes opened wide, my heart started racing. It was as if someone had been watching my every move and listening to my inner thoughts and then explained it all on paper. It was the beginning of realizing I wasn't doing everything wrong. The results gave me language for how and why I interact with the world naturally. It explained how and why people lived differently; why we had different areas of interest; why we would emphasize, prioritize, appreciate, get agitated by information or circumstances so differently.

I felt like someone permitted me to see the truth about how I am wired and said; "Be yourself."

An insight that speaks to our core being, longing, motivation, struggles, strengths and shadow side informs our self-awareness. Self-awareness leads to self-acceptance. I recommend doing this work, taking these assessments as they have also expanded my view of God and influenced my understanding and acceptance of others.

Read 1 Corinthians 12

Observe what is the same and what is different.
Record what you observe about God and the Holy Spirit.
Record what you observe about spiritual gifts.

> *"Each person is given something to do to show who God is." (I Corinthians 12: 6, The Message)*

What gift do you believe you've been given by the Spirit?
What does this passage tell you about who you are?
Is there a change to be made in your behavior, perspective, or understanding as you listen to this passage?

Pay Attention Practice Three

You love.

Read I Corinthians 13:3-7 out loud:

> *"If I give everything I own to the poor and even go to the stake to be burned as a martyr, but I don't love, I've gotten nowhere. So, no matter what I say, what I believe, and what I do, I'm bankrupt without love.*
> *Love never gives up.*
> *Love cares more for others than for self.*
> *Love doesn't want what it doesn't have.*
> *Love doesn't strut,*
> *Doesn't have a swelled head,*
> *Doesn't force itself on others,*
> *Isn't always "me first,"*
> *Doesn't fly off the handle,*
> *Doesn't keep score of the sins of others,*
> *Doesn't revel when others grovel,*
> *Takes pleasure in the flowering of truth,*
> *Puts up with anything,*
> *Trusts God always,*
> *Always looks for the best,*
> *Never looks back,*
> *But keeps going to the end.*
> *(1 Corinthians 13: 3-7 The Message)*

Love is a feeling. Love is a verb. Love is the most important way. Love God, and others as yourself is the highest calling and the signature of God believers, Jesus followers, and Holy Spirit-filled saints.

Review the top 20 list you made about yourself. Review what you observed about your spiritual gift(s) from yesterday. Using the following prompts with the list of how love acts from I Corinthians 13, write out questions about how to love yourself.

How do I
Where have I
Who needs me to
When do I
What makes me
Where will I
How can I

Example: When do I fly off the handle?
How can I use my gift of hospitality to put someone else first?

Let your questions be your prayers. Listen now and beyond your time today for answers. Record answers to your questions as they come.

Pay Attention Practice Four

You are changed and changing.

> *"My old self has been crucified with Christ. It is no longer I who live, but Christ lives in me. So I live in this earthly body by trusting in the Son of God, who loved me and gave himself for me" (Galatians 2: 20).*

A radical transformation is happening. Our old life died. A new life has been given to us. It will be completed not because we follow through on what was started, but because God promised He will do the finishing.

> *"There has never been the slightest doubt in my mind that the God who started this great work in you would keep at it and bring it to a flourishing finish on the very day Christ Jesus appears" (Philippians 1:6 The Message).*

> *"And this is the secret: Christ lives in you" (Colossians 1:27).*

The secret changes everything because it makes the impossible possible. Image-bearers, learn to participate in the work of being made new. Colossians 3 gives clarity to what it means to Live Wide Awake.

In your journal draw two horizontal lines, dividing a page into three sections. At the top of the first section put the word Record. At the top of the second section put the word Reflect. At the top of the third section put the word Respond.

Read Colossians 3 out loud or listen to it.

Record: What do you see, hear, wonder?

Reflect: What is the Living Word telling me about God? What does the Living Word say about me?

Respond: Was there a call to obedience, to confess and make a change, to get help to battle a part of the old nature that has a grip on you? Was there a shift in attitude to embrace, to extend forgiveness, or to pursue a new way of life?

Friends, I pray you can love who you are and dare to be fully yourself through the power of Christ Jesus who lives in you.

Pay Attention Practice Five

You belong.

One of the phrases my girls passed on to me from their time in nursing school was this: "Everybody is somebody's somebody." This speaks to connection and belonging and significance. It is profound to me that I am one of God's somebody's, somebody of great importance, somebody God knows intimately and loves perfectly. I am certain of this because I am a child of God.

> *"But to all who believed him and accepted him, he gave the right to become children of God. They are reborn - not with a physical birth resulting from human passion or plan, but a birth that comes from God" (John 1: 12-13).*

When you describe who you are, do you say you are a child of God? If not, why not? If yes, how does that influence the way you treat yourself?

Read through Galatians 3:23- 4:7 three times thoughtfully, as if you are a baker making a complex recipe for the first time.

First read through, listen for a word or phrase that sounds significant.

The second time through, read out loud and listen for repeated words. Write down the repeated words.

Third, read slowly listening for what the Living Word wants you to hear specifically.

Finish today in prayer by addressing God as Abba--the word a child uses when speaking to their daddy. Tell him why you're grateful to be His child. Talk to Him about the words that stood out, the message specific to you. Ask Him your questions about the repeated words if you don't understand them. Because you are a child of God, be as bold, as vulnerable, as authentic as possible in your spoken or written prayer.

Let The Word Walk

Do you know anyone who is struggling with identity? Share with them one truth you took from this chapter. As always, share the good news in your own words.

Meditation on Loving Who You Are

Sometimes we need practical tools to love ourselves for who we truly are. We are image-bearers of God, children by birth, children by faith, and His masterpiece loved perfectly. My friend Adie Johnson wrote a meditation based on Corinthians 13:4-10. It is a helpful tool for training us to love who we are. Healthy self-awareness, acceptance, and appreciation naturally leads to a healthy awareness, acceptance, and appreciation of others.

I've come back to this many times in my life, and I know the Lord uses it to speak comforting words to me. The Living Word is the best guide for living as one who is loved like crazy. That love is too much to contain, isn't meant to be hoarded, and can be offered generously to those we come into contact with.

May you speak it, pray it, live into it, and be abundantly blessed.

Meditation on Loving Yourself

When I love myself unconditionally, my love endures and I am patient and kind to myself.

When I love myself unconditionally, my love is never envious of others' bodies, relationships, possessions, or even character.

When I love myself unconditionally, my love never boils over with jealousy or self-hate. It is not boastful, and I don't have to show off to get attention. I am not conceited, but instead, know how to care for myself as well as others.

When I love myself unconditionally, my love is not rude to myself or someone else I might be intimidated by or jealous of.

When I love myself unconditionally, my love does not act unbecomingly. It does not insist on its rights or its own way, it is not self-seeking. It is self-caring.

When I love myself unconditionally, my love is not touchy, overly sensitive, fretful, or resentful. It doesn't keep score or hold grudges.

When I love myself unconditionally, my love doesn't beat me up for a word I wish I hadn't said or for an action I wish I had done.

When I love myself unconditionally, my love does not rejoice at injustice, to others or myself. My love rejoices when right and truth prevail. My love celebrates when I show up fully present, comfortable in my skin, able to offer the whole of who I am to life and the world.

I have learned that God's Love never fails, never fades out or becomes obsolete or comes to an end. And as a child of God, that love toward me never runs dry.

As for prophecy it will be fulfilled and pass away; as for tongues, they will be destroyed and cease; as for knowledge, it will pass away.

For our knowledge in this life is incomplete and imperfect, and our prophecy is fragmentary.

But when the complete and perfect understanding of love comes, the incomplete and imperfect will vanish away.

And I will dwell in God's unending, passionate love for me.

GOD IS

Peanut Butter Toast

Me, the mother, during dinner the first week of middle school: "Girls, what did you talk about in school today?"

Thing Two, the second of the twins, born one minute after the first, replied with disgust: "Peanut Butter Toast."

JR, the father: "Are you taking a cooking class?"

Thing One: "No. *You know*, peanut butter toast..."

Me, after looking with a furrowed brow at the father: "What class did you talk about peanut butter toast in?"

Thing Two: "Science class. We were talking about how sea life mates."

JR and I were utterly confused.

Thing One: "You know, Mom, when you told us how babies are made for the first time? Lauren said you made her eat peanut butter toast while she was listening, and she gagged. So that is what we call "it": Peanut Butter Toast."

Ha. Yes, I did make her eat the toast, because we were going on a hike afterward. I did not realize that her gagging and not wanting to eat was connected to her hearing about sex for the first time.

It took a while before Thing Two could eat peanut butter toast again. We still laugh about how we renamed what people generally refer to as "the birds and the bees."

I got to be the first one to have a conversation with my girls about sex before they heard confusing information about it. I got to lay the foundation of ongoing conversations about body image, body changes, body differences, and the incredible ways our bodies were designed to begin, grow, heal, perform, rest, and make babies.

I wonder what your experience was when you heard about sex for the first time.

This chapter is not about sex. It is about foundations--the base layer of understanding what you know and how or where you learned what you know. We're going to reflect on who God is, on the foundation he spoke into existence. You will get to think about who laid the groundwork, where it was laid, and what was said that began informing your knowledge of Father God, Jesus, and the Holy Spirit.

Pay Attention Practice One

Look at the artwork at the beginning of this section.

"God Is…"
What words would you use to finish that statement?

> *"First, God. God is the subject of life. God is the foundation for living. If we don't have a sense of the primacy of God, we will never get it right, get life right, get our lives right. Not God at the margins; not God as an option; not God on the weekends. God at the center and circumference; God first and last; God, God, God"*
>
> **Eugene Peterson**[10]

Who told you about God for the first time?
What is the first thing you learned about God?
When did you learn about Jesus?
How was Jesus introduced to you?
What helped you initially understand the Holy Spirit?
How does Father, Son, and Spirit fit into the foundation of your faith?
Do you believe without having seen that God brought creation and created beings into existence out of nothing and by his creative Word?

Let the questions be prompts for you to write the foundation of how you know about God and how you've come to know God personally.

Is the initial foundation strong? Does it have any gaps?

Pay Attention Practice Two

Who is God? That is a question to ponder for a lifetime. It's an important one to be able to answer in the now, even though your answer will change as you get to know God more. He is knowable. I believe our understanding eventually leads us to a place where we can answer with certainty, humility, and contentment that God is impossible to fully define with our intellect, analogies, experiences, denominational theology, or our carefully-crafted words.

I encourage you to go to the place God is introduced. Let the perfect beginning establish a foundation for who God is.

"Time in erodes awareness of."

Andy Stanley, Deep and Wide[11]

If you are familiar with Genesis one and two, I suggest you read through these chapters out loud or listen to the passage. It is common for words to go flat after years of reading something over and over. Scripture was originally spoken to listeners, not read by readers. Hearing it will help bring a new awareness of this remarkable, almost unbelievable telling of the beginning of creation, but more importantly the beginning of God revealing Himself to us.

Read out loud or listen to Genesis 1 and 2

What does Genesis reveal about God?
What is remarkable about the world?
What does it say about you?
Is there anything that surprises you?
Is there anything that is hard to believe?

What do you learn about the love of God?
Did you hear anything that fills in gaps you had from your initial understanding of God?
Did you have questions about creation or the creator?

Pay Attention Practice Three

On a blank piece of paper center this title at the top:
GOD SAID, AND THAT IS WHAT HAPPENED

Next, draw a horizontal line to divide the paper in half. Then draw two lines from the top of the page to the bottom to create six equal boxes. Each box represents one day of creation.

Read Genesis 1:3-27
In each box list what God spoke into creation with as many descriptors as you find. You might find it helpful to read Genesis 1 in multiple translations. If you only have one, go to biblegateway.com and choose several translations or paraphrases that you don't have at home.

Make up a poem, a song, an acronym, an acrostic, rhyme, or rap, that will help you remember the order of creation. If you have kids in your life, teach them your creative way to remember.

When God is done speaking something or someone into existence what does He do? What does He think? How does He feel about his work?

Pay Attention Practice Four

There is more creation detail in Genesis two. There are two lavish gifts created we tend to overlook. One is the gift of time, the other the gift of place.

Read Genesis two. Record what was completed, what was created, what had not happened, and what had already happened.

Record the needs of creation, the needs of humans, and the provision of the Creator.

Connect the story of the created world to your current world. Where do you see God's presence in your present circumstances; world issues and current needs?

> *"God doesn't work impersonally from space; he works with us where we are, as he finds us. No matter what we do, whether good or bad, we continue to be part of everything that God is doing"*
>
> **Eugene Peterson**[12]

Pay Attention Practice Five

Spend time in Creation. Get out there in the sun, rain, or wind. Sit on the grass or a rock with your back up against a tree. Don't speak, just listen and observe anything you hear that is God-made, not man-made. As you notice those sounds, thank God. Observe the temperature and textures you feel. Touch God-made things. When you feel them, tell God Thank You. Notice what you smell and thank God for every scent. For every single, God-made thing you see, specifically Thank God for that.

Finish by telling God out loud what you think about His creation.

Remember, God loved us in his creating of us. He poured out his favor on all He created. He did that first, before we loved him. God never stops loving. God loved us before we could do anything good or anything bad. God's love is complete. We have it all. We cannot do something to make him love us more or make him love us less. God didn't only love us that one time a long time ago. His love for you and me is an active presence living in us.

Let the Word Walk

When you are at the table with friends or family, ask them about their first introduction to God. Who told them? What were they told about Jesus? What were their first impressions of the Holy Spirit? What were their first questions?

Go Deeper

Spend some time thinking and journaling about the seventh day:

Do any questions come up when you read Genesis 2:2-3?

Where did you first learn about Sabbath?

Do you think Sabbath is a gift, a religious rule, an outdated tradition, necessary or reasonable in modern life, or something else altogether?

Is a day of rest and play something you practice? If so, how do you practice it?

If thinking about Sabbath sparks curiosity, bring it up as a table topic next time you're eating with other people. Listen to the history people have with it, their understanding of it, their appreciation for it, or their dismissal of it.

God Can Do Anything You Know

JR and I have been married for over thirty years. In year twenty-five, we renewed our vows under a Maui sunset. The event was officiated by Rev Alapaki and witnessed by our twin daughters and my parents. Rev Alapaki sang a Hawaiian blessing on us as we agreed to covenant again. We spoke words of affirmation and blessing to our teenage daughters, then sang the Lord's prayer in thankful harmony to God who brought us together. My verbal promise to JR went something like this: "I will go where you go; your people will be my people."

The spring following our Maui remarriage, JR told me he was applying for a position that could move us to Florida from Colorado. I would go with him wherever he was going.

The application turned into an offer. I was faithful to my promise, so we sold our Colorado home and moved to a temporary dwelling in Boca Raton, Florida. We planned to explore the area before settling into our next mortgage.

My father-in-law Bob wisely pointed out that it is one thing to talk about moving and change and adventure over a cocktail months before it happens, but it is a completely different matter when you are starting to count down the days. It's another reality altogether when you actually arrive in the land of everything new.

Freak-out moments were husband approved, "as long as we're not having them at the same time." He clarified, "Someone has to keep their feet on the ground, pointed forward, holding tightly to the hand of the one wanting to run back toward familiar land."

I decided to face change and the unknown. I chose to let go and move ahead, to grieve the loss of knowing and being known and embrace new opportunities with an attitude of adventure.

The cocktail conversations were over. The time came to lace up my moving shoes, figure out how to plug-in and steady a crockpot in a moving RV, cancel cable, give people a forwarding address, and watch the Grabel packers take our stuff away in boxes.

We loaded Calvin the dog and Pekoe the cat into the Cruise America RV and set off into the unknown roads, toward unknown places, to meet the unknown people in Florida.

Six months into South Florida living, the work environment got weird. When any organization is toxic, it cannot be covered up for long. Six months later, ten days before closing on a townhouse, things went from weird to downright wrong. JR walked in the door after work one evening, threw down some papers on the kitchen table, and said, "That's it. I'm pushing the eject button."

What the papers said was devastating. His job title changed. His pay rate decreased. His responsibilities shrunk. The large plant in his office was exchanged for a smaller one. JR's response was warranted.

I just said, "Okay."

We ate dinner without tasting, without words. When we finished I started reading numbly. Each night after dinner we had been reading out of Isaiah in The Message. That night we were in chapter 40. We have a version of The Message that has commentary included by Eugene Peterson. This is what Pastor Peterson wrote to help us hear what God was saying through Isaiah:

"That is to say, don't build castles in the air, don't construct an elaborate fantasy life about God's future for you. In the desert, prepare the way of the Lord. Right here, where the going is roughest. Here, in a foreign place. Here, in exile.

> *"In this passage, the geographical present is emphasized. This very dry, colorless, arid existence that seems to characterize the life of the sufferer--here is where the highway of God is to be built. Don't look for some ejection button to push for an immediate escape. Instead build a highway, which takes time. Build it well. And build it where you are"*
>
> **Eugene Peterson**[13]

JR was shocked by those specific words.

At that moment I'm positive that's not what we expected nor wanted to hear. It was unmistakably clear God was talking. So, we did the best we could to stay where we were at, to make a highway. We stayed for nearly two more years. It was hard. Nearly all our appliances broke, one at a time. A rat went through all our cabinets and did its nasty business. A car accident broke our daughter's hand and totaled our car. Our house payment increased by $700 without warning. Those types of circumstances felt like rugs being pulled out from under our feet, relentlessly. Simultaneously, God sent amazing humans for us to love and be loved by during those rough years in that foreign place. They were comforting. They were fun. We shared mutual need and benevolence. We were not alone.

On our refrigerator, we posted these words: "God can do anything you know" (Ephesians 3:20 The Message). Those words stayed on the fridge until the morning we left Florida.

That message is true. I've lived it. I see it in our story, hear it in your stories, read it in so many stories recorded in the Living Word. In hindsight, I know that we were meant to be where we were, not because it was a good fit, but because God made a way for us to go, told us to stay, and released us to leave when the time was right. I do not have to understand it all. He did big work in us there.

I now refer to that time as our "wilderness by the sea." Wilderness adventure reveals weakness. It requires more than resilience. Wilderness living is a training ground where change takes place. I was taken from places and people I knew, roles I had, and hats I wore that were comfortable and familiar. Moving to Florida was a transition into isolation, and it was disorienting. JR apologized often for bringing us there, doubting that his decision to leave Colorado was the right one. He commented often that people didn't know the true JR in Florida, because he felt perpetually discouraged, trapped, and wasn't himself. Change always involves loss. That's why people don't want change and don't want to change. Loss of identity or someone you love, loss of position, power, or material possessions, and loss of relationship status or healthy physical condition are unwelcome events in anyone's life. What God changes in us when we're in a "wilderness" place is transforming too. He brings new life, new freedom, deeper trust, stronger faith, sweet peace, and true joy.

During our wilderness by the sea, we became acutely aware God is enough. He is more than enough.

Honestly, if all we depended on was our weak strength and limited understanding, we would have ejected. Thank goodness God is strong, kind, and clear enough for us to stay on the adventure he calls us to.

Practice Attention Practice One

Isaiah 40 is Good News. Isaiah was a prophet for about 50 years, during the reign of four different Kings. He spoke into the future lives and the present times of God's people. He warned them, cast visions, called out rebellious behavior, and spread hope. The people needed what was said then. People haven't changed much. I believe we need the same message now.

We are likely to fail, fall in love with idols, and unravel ourselves and organizations and neighborhoods and governments. We fight, rebel, collapse, and cry out. God still gathers people, lives among them, delivers them, leads them, provides for them, reveals himself to them, and calls his people to come and humble themselves. He teaches us to depend on Him.

We will only trust a God we know. Often, our ideas of God and our carefully-constructed confines of God blow up when life throws us into suffering and distress. The well-controlled faith system doesn't hold up when life doesn't make sense. Deconstruction of what we were comfortable with can lead to a reconstructed, intimate relationship with the God of love.

This passage begins with Isaiah sending a message of hope to people in the thick of adversity. There is a call to trust at the end which looks like waiting, looks like faith in the thick of it.

Because I am acquainted with loss, trauma, and seasons of significant change, I tend to live in expectation of the next horrible situation. I am certain God would much prefer I live with a confident expectation that He is good and loves me like crazy.

We all need the good news of Isaiah 40. We all need to soak in the bold words Isaiah spoke about our God of love.

Read Isaiah 40.

Choose several days in a row to read this passage. I suggest four or more.

Each day, choose a different way to read meaning:

Listen to it.
Write it out.
Read it in your favorite translation.
Read it in a different translation.
Read it out loud.
Pay attention to how God speaks through Isaiah into your present circumstances and in your journal, record what God is saying.

Pay Attention Practice Two

Meditate on Isaiah 40.

Can you identify and admit to at least one thing you do regularly that is a time-waster? Here is a challenge that has the potential to change your day and, if practiced, your life:

Give up one thing you waste time on during the days you choose to read this passage. Use that time to meditate on this passage.

Start this practice by imagining you and Isaiah are close friends. You meet for a glass of wine and half-price appetizers every week at your favorite spot in town. Since you were in the audience when Isaiah said these things you want to use your weekly happy hour to pepper him with questions. Ask as many as you can.

Write down your questions.

Pay Attention Practice Three

Pray Isaiah 40: 28-31.

In spoken or written form, talk to Jesus by borrowing the words of Isaiah to pray the Scripture.

Claim the promises for yourself and others. Bring distress or suffering to Jesus. Pray the problems, not the solution. Praise God, starting with all that is describing Him here and for all the reasons you know He deserves to be praised.

Pay Attention Practice Four

Live Isaiah 40.

Before you read Isaiah 40 today, start with this prayer:

Lord God Almighty, the one who calls out and calls by name every single star, I stand in awe of you. I believe you see my troubles, the troubles of the world. I believe you care and want what is best for your people. Help me be observant when I read your Word today. I want to understand how to apply it to my life.

What stands out in your reading today?

How can you work what you have heard into your life? Since living is dynamic, change happens. Change = loss, which makes sense of our avoidance of dealing with it.

Here are some questions to ponder with regard to desired change. Be honest in your answers.

Is there any change happening in your life?
Is there something that needs to change?
Is someone else changing something that affects you?
Are you leading change in some aspect of life?
How do you respond to or react to change?
What loss will occur in connection to current or anticipated change?
Is there anything you haven't let go of that will allow the change to take place?
Can you let God be enough for you in this change?

Is there anything helpful in Isaiah 40 you can live into?

Let the Word Walk

I have yet to meet anyone who doesn't need encouragement. Would you be willing to share some of the good news you've gotten from this chapter with someone who needs it? If you don't know who to share with, ask the Lord to tell you.

Go Deeper

The word Gospel means good news. There is a beautiful connection between the good news in Isaiah 40 and the New Testament Gospels.

Verses 3-5 are quoted in all four gospels.
Matthew 3:3, Mark 1:1-11; Luke 3: 4-6; John 1: 23

Read Isaiah 40:3-5 followed by one or all of the passages in the New Testament.

What connections do you see? What does that say about who God is? Why does that matter to you?

Becoming A Mother

There was only one thing that I knew for sure I wanted to do when I grew up: be a mom. My mother often shared a funny tale of wanting to have ten children and then, when she had me, she changed the number to five. I have chosen to spin that in my favor, understanding her to mean having me gave her the satisfaction of six children, so she only needed four more. I never wanted ten or even five kids, but I knew for sure I wanted to be a mother.

I married JR in July, 1986. By August, I was ready to start a family. JR suggested we would benefit from learning to be married for a while first. The following year I brought up having a baby again. JR bought me a puppy to help me wait another year. In 1990, after years of trying to start a family with little success month after month, after buckets of tears and fountains of frustration, after bargaining and begging with God, I was pregnant.

With triplets.

Imagine if you found out that in a matter of months you would go from having no children to three infants. Really, stop a minute and just let your mind go there. I don't remember all of what I thought about initially, but I am certain I never thought about what it would be like to say hello and goodbye to those three infants in the same day.

At twenty-three weeks and five days, we delivered Calvin, Leah, and Andrew. They cried. They had the tiniest fingers and toes. They were baptized. They lived, and then died, in our arms.

No one could have prepared me for being a mother that would bury her first three children. I never had this scenario in mind. I didn't want to be a grieving mother. I wanted a baby to love and care for. I wanted to raise a child.

I won't ask you to imagine what it's like to bury a child. Some of you reading this already know. Others know similar unexpected and devastating loss. This unsettled every part of my being, including my faith. Grieving was deep, grueling, and long.

About six months into that grief I shook my fist at the sky, and fiercely screamed, "If you are for real, God, what do you want with me?"

I stood at a critical crossroad. One way was a choice of bitterness. The other was the way of joy. I was prepared for bitterness, prepared to let go of believing in God. I was ready to live a dark, inward, hard-hearted, shut-down existence. But there must have been hope, too. It must have been quietly pleading behind the pain.

I stood in a field, my dog next to me, and shouted. Immediately I heard this in response: "I want all of you."

Though the words were not loud, they were clear. Though I didn't understand the words, I heard them. Though I knew they were from the One, I knew I didn't know this One like I thought I did. He spoke to me.

God answered my question in a way I think my dog might have heard, in a way you might have heard if you were standing in that field with me. The words gave me the courage to choose the way of joy.

In the hospital room after receiving the news we would deliver the babies and that it was not possible to perform life-saving measures, my husband and I were left alone for a while. We looked at one another in disbelief, then started to say these words we later had to look up. They were the words of Psalm 121. I believe God spoke into our hearts in that intense moment to let us know He was very present. I believe He did the same in that field where I stood with my dog.

And so many years later, I believe His words were not for me alone. They were for you, too. You who might be currently devastated, desperate, or in the midst of grueling grief or pain, the Lord is present. He wants all of you, too.

Pay Attention Practice One

Read Psalm 121.
What do you hear as the main emphasis of this psalm?

Read it a second time out loud. Write down the words that stand out to you on a notecard and repeat them, chew on them, wonder why they stood out. Carry the notecard with you this week, or put the verse in your Reminder app on your phone. It will pop up for you to see, memorize, and meditate on all week.

NOTE: Meditate doesn't mean just sitting quietly with the Bible open on your lap, coffee in your hand, reading. It means to chew, taste, swallow, and chew the words some more. I like the image that Eugene Peterson shares of meditation being like a dog gnawing on a bone, coming at it from all angles, and focusing attention on savoring.

Pay Attention Practice Two

"Because old Mother Nature is a dysfunctional parent who keeps sending us mixed messages, we need both faith and doubt. The birth of every infant whispers of a God who loves stories; the death of every infant calls his existence into question."

John Ortberg from Faith and Doubt[14]

When I heard the words, "I want all of you," I didn't understand what they meant. I also didn't know who said them to me. The God I had known about all my life wasn't one who would speak out loud or respond so specifically. I did not know this God. I've had a few years to ponder these words in my heart and figure out what it means to live like that. One truth that Psalm 121 points out is that I am someone who needs help. God wants the parts of me that need help. He told me loud and clear He is my help. It has taken many years to learn to take my need for help to God before I take it to another human being.

Think about the word 'help' and answer the following questions:

Who do you go to for help?
Who do you help?
How do you help others?
What part of you needs help?
Will you ask for help? If not, why not?
How has God helped you in the past?
What helps you live as a healthy version of yourself?
What do others do to help you live wide awake?

What help do you seek from God to live wide awake?
What doubts do you have about God's help?
What other questions would you write for this pay attention practice about the help of God?

Write out Psalm 121, inserting your name in place of 'you' or 'Israel.' Read it out loud as a prayer.

Pay Attention Practice Three

God spoke. I am one hundred percent certain that the voice I heard was the voice of God himself. I didn't see anyone. I didn't see a bright light, angels, fire, or anything I can't describe. God is present. His presence was there. His presence is here, now. A practice I like to use to help me focus or settle down is to sit quietly in a comfortable place where I won't be disturbed. Sometimes I set a timer for five or ten minutes. Then I use these words in a form of prayer: "Father, let me be present to your Presence."

Begin with the presence prayer. It might be helpful to whisper the prayer out loud. Address God in the way most natural for you. When the prayer time is over, finish by reading Psalm 103: 1-5. out loud, borrowing David's words of thanks.

> *"Let all that I am praise the Lord;*
> *with my whole heart, I will praise his Holy name.*
> *Let all that I am praise the Lord;*
> *may I never forget all the good things he does for me.*
> *He forgives all my sins*
> *and heals all my diseases.*
> *He redeems me from death*
> *and crowns me with love and tender mercies.*
> *He fills my life with good things. My youth is renewed like the eagle's!"*
> *(Psalm 103:1-5)*

I am sure David had specifics in mind when he was referring to the "good things" God had done for him.

Do you believe God is good?

If you're not sure you believe in a good God right now, list specific reasons why. Be honest with God, who knows your heart.

If you answered yes, reflect on and write down what good things you can identify in the past week, in the past month, and in the past year.

Make a list, make art, make music as a way to not forget all the good things, and praise God with all of yourself today.

Pay Attention Practice Four

Read through Psalm 103 slowly.
Read it again in The Message.

Specific revelations of God's character are all over this Psalm. Divide a page horizontally. At the top of the page write, "God's Good Things." Fill up that half of the page with what David lists as blessings of a good God.

At the top of the bottom half of the page write, "Remember." Write out all or a part of this Psalm that speaks to something your inmost being needs to know, be reminded of, or let sink in.

Verse one speaks to our different words in different translations:

"all that I am" (NLT)
"with my whole heart" (NLT)
"my soul" (NIV, KJ, The Message)
"from head to toe" (The Message)
"all my inmost being" (NIV)
"all that is within me" (NASB, NKJ)
"all my inward parts" (Youngs Literal Translation)

What do those words mean to you?
Can you identify any part of you that does not engage with God?

Pay Attention Practice Five

Sometimes I can read the Living Word as if I am sitting in my lazy-girl chair scrolling through Instagram. Reading that way makes it possible to get up and walk away without having absorbed much. I encourage you to read today's passage like you're a well-respected baker trying out a new recipe that you will sell in your bakery later in the day. You need to pay close attention to all the details.

Today's passage was written by Paul, whose life story is filled with suffering that he caused and experienced. I hope you have not expected that having a relationship with God would exempt you from hassles, hard times, or adversity while we're here on Earth. I may have believed some version of that when I was younger, but at this point I am embracing how the rough patches belong as much as the healing from those rough patches. I'm aware of how celebration and sorrow can co-exist and Christ is everywhere. This is a way I understand God wanting 'all of me' in those places, not just after they're over.

Read 2 Corinthians 4 and 2 Corinthians 5:7
As if you were writing out a recipe, take a verse or two at a time and record what is important as if it were an ingredient list for a recipe. Try to write it in your own words.

On the side of the list, record any word or concept you don't understand.

When you are done with the 'ingredient' list, write down a summary of this chapter the same way the baker would write out instructions for the ingredients.

What is true about Paul?

What does this say about God?
What is the message for all believers?
Is there a personal insight for you?
Do you have an action item to respond to?

Finally, give this 'recipe' (chapter) a title. It will help you remember and be able to refer to it later. And maybe, you will want to share it with someone else!

Let The Word Walk

Be intentional to let what the Word worked in your heart now work in your world. Tell one person one thing that you received, wondered about, learned, were comforted by, convinced of, or helped by this week.

Going Deeper

There are two options for this chapter.

1. Here are four big words used to encompass the marvelous, mysterious God of love. They are words to help you grasp why and how God is able to help everyone in any situation, with any need.

Omniscient—God knows perfectly and eternally everything that can be known.

Omnipotent—All-powerful. God can do whatever He wills and cannot do anything contrary to His nature.

Omnipresent—God "fills the universe in all its parts and is present everywhere at once. Not a part, but the whole of God is present in every place."[15]

Omni-benevolent—God is perfectly good. He is the source of all goodness. All creatures benefit from his generosity and kindness. His all-good character is seen in giving and forgiving.

Address each word with these three questions:

What does this mean to me?
What does this mean for everyone, everywhere, all the time?
How does this matter in my life?

Record questions that arise. These are concepts that enlarge beliefs and understanding.

Record what is comforting, convincing, or clarifying.

2. Psalm 46 is another Song worth meditating on. It was Martin Luther's inspiration when he wrote *A Mighty Fortress is our God.* The Psalm is song of hope when people need help. The emphasis of this chapter of the book, is for us to know who God is. He is not absent when life is hard. I'm not alone when I say hard times lead to deeper experiences of the power of God, the love of Jesus, and the ability to hear the Holy Spirit's voice.

Using the following words to begin, write out your own question based on this Psalm and search for the answer.

Who
What
Where
When
How
Why

Example: What am I afraid of?

Oh You Love Me Like That

My dad worked for IBM for thirty-two years. Because of his employer, we moved a lot, and each time it was usually far away from where we had previously lived. One time when I was in college, I stayed behind in South Dakota and the rest of my family moved to Colorado. There, my parents fell in love with a young man named JR DeGroot. They agreed this young man would fit nicely into their family, which translated into strategic planning to get me to notice the young man so we could fall in love and get married. Their efforts were successful, though I will admit I was slow to understand how JR felt about me until a night under the full moon.

JR picked me up from the airport and drove me to his house, where my car sat completely detailed, inside and out. Even the engine was clean. The shiny car surprise was just the beginning. A cassette tape of Chicago 17, a romantic card, and a rose accompanied this unmistakable expression of his feelings. I received each token one at a time, slowly catching on that he was trying to tell me something. And then, he kissed me under a full moon.

"Oh, you like me like *that*," I said.

We were married a year later. Yes, Mom, you may have all the credit.

Fifteen years later I found a stack of yellow lined paper folded up in squares. I began unfolding and discovered love letters on legal paper, written by JR when I first moved from college to Colorado as he was falling in love with me. I was in a new town, and only knew my family. I left college in a bad place, hanging out with people who were bad for me. I was not making good life decisions. I was not healthy physically, emotionally, or spiritually. I was not looking for love, and I did not think I was lovable. I refer to that time as "the stupid year." I am certain I did not absorb the message in these letters when I first received them. Now, I laughed, cried, and shook my head in the realization that JR fell in love with me at my *worst*. On the floor with those legal paper love letters, I suddenly, clearly heard these words:

> *"But God demonstrated His great love for us in that while we were yet sinners, Christ died for us" (Romans 5:8)*

"Oh. You love me like *that*," I said to Jesus. And I wept.

Do you know how dearly loved you are? Are you aware you are one of God's treasured possessions? You are, sweet child of God, you are. JR expressed love to me that I hadn't experienced before. I was unfamiliar with romantic love, so I didn't recognize it right away. I did later.

If you are a fellow dog owner, you will be familiar with their affectionate, unconditional love. They demand very little in return.

Maybe you're familiar with the mutual companionship and respect of a close friend. The two of you are interested in and curious about the same things. You share laughter and sorrow over both lighthearted and significant circumstances. This friendship is defined by trust. This is another type of love.

The love of God shown to us in Jesus is a new kind of love that originates in God. The greek word for it is *agape*. Agape love is used in the Living Word to express the love God has for us, the love we have for God, and the spiritual love we can have toward other humans. God's love is permanent and powerful. God's love is characterized by giving and forgiving. It is expressed in compassion, tenderness, and empathy with the sufferings of humanity. To be familiar with this agape love is to know God.

My prayer for you as you engage with the Word in this chapter is the same as Paul's for his Ephesian friends.

> *"I pray that from his glorious, unlimited resources he will empower you with inner strength through his Spirit. Then Christ will make his home in your hearts as you trust in him. Your roots will grow down into God's love and keep you strong. And may you have the power to understand, as all God's people should, how wide, how long, how high, and how deep his love is. May you experience the love of Christ, though it is too great to understand fully. Then you will be made complete with all the fullness of life and power that comes from God." (Eph 3: 16-19)*

Meditate on it. Let it bother you, encourage you, startle you, convict you, delight you, and inspire you. The purpose of the Word is transformation. Be open to the God of love and the love of God.

Jesus Love

Dallas Willard wrote:

"Love means will-to-good, willing the benefit of what or who is loved. We may say we love chocolate cake, but we don't. Rather, we want to eat it. That is desire, not love. In our culture, we have a great problem distinguishing between love and desire, but it is essential that we do so. New Testament Greek has several words for "love." Two are eros

(from which we get "erotic") and agape. Agape love, perhaps the greatest contribution of Christ to human civilization, wills the good of whatever it is directed upon. It does not wish to consume it. The teaching about love that still permeates Western civilization in its better moments understands that."[16]

"The key to understanding this and other statements about love is to know that this love (the Greek word agape) is not so much a matter of emotion as it is of doing things for the benefit of another person, that is, having an unselfish concern for another and a willingness to seek the best for another."[17]

In these Pay Attention practices, I want you to see the way the love of God through Jesus "wills-the-good" toward people. Listen to Jesus's willingness to "seek the best for another." The ways and the words might surprise you. I hope you find yourself saying, "Oh, you love me like that!"

Remember, God is unchanging.

Pay Attention Practice One

I've been to the Grand Canyon. I've been to the Colorado Rocky Mountains. I've been to Kenya. I met Eugene Peterson. I met Emily P. Freeman. I had coffee one-on-one with Don Postema. I've been married for 33 years to JR DeGroot. I am the mother of Joyful Lauren and Gracious Lyndsay. I received second runner up in a Junior Miss Pageant. I earned an all-expenses-paid trip to Paris for two. I won tacos for a year by being the right caller on a radio show.

All of these places, people, and experiences are significant parts of my life--some more significant than others. If you are patient enough to listen to all my animated stories you would get a sense of how great all these people and places were.

John 3 is a bit like Jesus telling us about somewhere, someone, something more magnificent than any of us could imagine yet none of us have experienced. Bring your patient, attentive self to this chapter, because you are about to hear Jesus himself tell you what the love of God is and who the God of love is. Set yourself up to listen as if Jesus is looking directly at you, saying: There is something really special I want to tell you.

Read John 3: 1-21 as if you were out on a walk at night and sat down for a few minutes to enjoy the cool evening and gorgeous moon. You see Jesus and Nicodemus meeting up at the park, too. You decide to stay where you are and listen in on their conversation. What stands out?

Read it again out loud. This time, imagine you are Nicodemus coming to Jesus one-on-one because you want to understand who He is.

Did you hear anything by reading it out loud that you haven't heard before?

Read John 3:16-17 inserting your name.

Read the passage again, inserting the name of someone you love but are concerned about.

Finally, insert the name of a person, president, professor, pastor, friend, foe, adversary, employer, student, significant other, or someone else different than you. God loved the world so much He sent Jesus to save us and The Holy Spirit to give us new, eternal life. He loves us like that.

Does that make sense to you? It didn't to Nicodemus, so Jesus made it incredibly clear that the love of God is incredibly close. Jesus seeks the best for another in his words to Nicodemus.

Pay Attention Practice Two

Read John 8.
Pay attention to details in this story by investigating:

Where it took place
What time it was
Who was there
How individuals or groups of people react to Jesus
Why did religious leaders do such a thing?

Read the story from the perspective of the man who is gripping the arm of the woman and dragging her in front of Jesus.

What is your reaction to Jesus' response?

Read the story again from the perspective of the woman.

What is your reaction to Jesus' response?
What does the love of Jesus look like in this story?

Pay Attention Practice Three

Enter your time with the Living Word prayerfully. Here is a prayer to begin your time:

> *"Gracious and loving God, you know the deep inner patterns of my life that keep me from being totally yours. You know the misinformed structures of my being that hold me in bondage to something less than your high purpose for my life. You also know my reluctance to let you have your way with me in these areas. Hear the deeper cry of my heart for wholeness and by your grace enable me to be open to your transforming presence in this reading.*
> *Lord, have mercy" (Robert Mulholland).*[18]

Read John 13: 1-17

Write down what Jesus said and did.

Maya Angelou said: "*I've learned that people will forget what you said, people will forget what you did, but people will never forget how you made them feel.*"[19]

Sit up in your chair with both feet on the floor. Look at your feet. Imagine they are dirty and bare, and you're about to wash them off in a bowl of warm, soapy water. Jesus comes to you with a towel over his shoulder, kneels by the bowl, takes your feet in his hands and washes them. He pours clean warm water over them to rinse them off. He puts your feet in his towel and dries them.

How do you feel?
How do you describe this love?

Do you want to say anything to Jesus? Write that down in a journal, on a notecard, or speak out loud so you can see and hear your response to the love of Jesus.

Oh yes, He loves us like *that*.

Pay Attention Practice Four

Prayer: Jesus, please open the eyes of my heart to see the wonderful truth of your agape love.

Read John 5. 1-20
Use your observational skills to identify:

Who, What, Where, When, Why and How. Come up with your own questions using each word at least once.

For example:

What do you think Jesus wanted people to know?
Why would he want them to know?

Write a title and a summary in your own words of this passage.

If you have time, read all of John 5. Highlight or write down what stands out as most applicable to your current circumstances.

Pay Attention Practice Five

We are generally better givers than receivers. Receiving words, gifts, actions, and expressions of love can be missed or misunderstood if we are not intentional about receiving. Before you engage with the Living Word of Love, please prepare yourself to receive. If your mind is already off in a thousand directions, your heart is weary, or your spirit is spooled up, this might *not* be the best time for you to receive. Maybe a walk, accomplishing a task, a nap, a sandwich, or a hot bath would be a better way to love yourself. Care for yourself first. You have permission to do so.

When you are ready to be intentional about receiving, here is a simple practice to prepare: Find a comfortable place to read. Close your eyes, then starting from the top of your head, relax each part of your body by taking a deep breath. When you slowly let the breath out, feel your head relax. On your next breath let your shoulders and back relax. Repeat with your arms, then your waist and hips, your legs, and finally your feet.

Read John 15: 1-17. Listen closely, and receive.

What is repeated?
What is emphasized?
What is compared?
What is the key or main message Jesus is making?
Write down what you wonder when you read Jesus words.

Do you believe God loves you like that?

How can you both receive the message and put it into action?

Let The Word Walk

Ask God to make you aware of someone who needs to know the love of Jesus in word, deed, prayer, or practical support. When He shows you, respond knowing you received the privilege of bringing a blessing to someone in the power and with the provision of God's love.

Going Deeper

How loved people love.

Read I John 4: 7-21

What words or phrases are repeated?
What is contrasted?

I am grateful to say I know or have known women and men who love others, who trust the God of love. The love of God lives in them. What a privilege to see, hear, and learn from how that love manifests itself. All of them would confess Jesus is the Son of God. They would all testify to the work and words of the Holy Spirit in ordinary and extraordinary circumstances. They are unique in age, ethnicity, gender, background, personality, life experiences, and vocation, yet they are similar in spirit. They are yielders, wrestlers, surrenderers. If you listened to them talk or watched them live, you would know how their common surrender landed them in the love John writes about here.

Who are those people in your life?

Read I John 4: 7-21 slowly a second time, out loud.

What do you hear about the love of God and the God of love that speaks to you specifically?

Take time to write to one of the yielders, wrestlers, surrenderers in your life. Be specific in your note about what they've done to make the love of God evident to you. Send the note too!

Live Wide Awake

Mission It's Possible

Today's story, about living wide awake, will be told by my friend of many years, Heidi Hoback. Her natural creativity, kindness, and compassion influenced the lives of children in our church community and the public school system. Heidi has been a Court Appointed Special Advocate volunteer for years, being both a companion and champion for children who experience neglect and abuse. Her heart is big, her generosity is expansive, her ability to sew and design beautiful things blesses the world around her.

My children and I were and still are recipients of Heidi's life. I've asked her to write the story of a group we were in together; a group of moms and daughters who got involved with other moms, daughters, women, and girls in kind, creative, and compassionate ways. She worked closely with another dear friend and powerful leader of all-things-kids, Pat Jones. Because they were a dynamic duo, I thought this story would be best told from Heidi's perspective.

In Memory of Pat Jones who showed us what it meant to Live Wide Awake

By Heidi Hoback

GEMS ended.

For years, our elementary and pre-teen girls met weekly in large and small groups. Through activities and conversations, they grew relationships with one another, their leaders and with Jesus. The club was called GEMS - Girls Everywhere Meeting the Savior. A rich and wonderful season of leading and participating brought girls and their moms together. We grew to know and love one another. When it was over, we collectively grieved the end of this special experience.

Our leader, Pat Jones, was known for brainstorming with God while jogging around the lake near her home. Following GEMS ending she jogged, listening for messages, looking for signs He may give her about what was to come next. She and God came up with an acronym for a new idea: MIP = Mission, It's Possible. For many years, I (Heidi) had been Pat's trusted assistant in GEMS and in Children's Ministry at a little church called Crestview in Boulder, Colorado. We fed off each other's zany ideas, brought complementary skills to the table, and laughed a lot. I was happy to be where Pat was, doing what she was doing.

Have you heard the saying: "Look for where God is at work and join in doing what He's doing?" That is where Pat looked and where Pat went, so I went too and we brought the rest of the girls and moms along with us. MIP began with a tiny girl from Haiti named Baby Darla. She was living with a host family in Pat's neighborhood and was in the US because she needed cleft palate surgery. We decided to help make that surgery possible with a fundraising event in her host family's small town. Our girls approached local businesses to ask for donations. Some baked pies. Others used sewing skills and made items to sell. The event was a huge success, and we reached our goal with a little leftover to start a bank account for our next project!

The next project was prompted by someone in that same town who worked at a local sewing shop. "Caps for Cancer" brought us together making warm fleece caps to give to women fighting cancer.

Word about our group got out and we were approached by a nurse-midwife who was going to go to Afghanistan to work with newborns. The MIP's got together and made baby blankets for her to deliver to the moms and babies. We called this mission: "Quilts for Kabul."

Later that summer, this same midwife came to us with a story about a woman who was homeless and pregnant that she met through a hospital program. The MIP's planned a baby shower with food and decorations. We bought and made gifts for God's new creation, Baby Terea. We held the shower in Denver's City Park and this time invited more families to join the celebration. Celebrating and holding Terea, sharing a meal and gifts with her mom whose life situation was very different than ours, powerfully affected us all.

God expanded our hearts and our mission when a friend of the group, Eileen, and her family began the process of adopting three sisters from Ukraine. She knew that a group of Ukranian children, all orphans of various ages, were scheduled to come to Colorado the following summer with hopes of finding new families. We pulled off a backyard carnival for the kids when they arrived. Despite the language barrier, our girls and the Ukranian children hit it off. What a joy for us all to share food, play, and laughter--a universal language.

Our final project brought us back to Baby Terea. Congregating again at City Park in Denver, we hosted Terea's first birthday party and witnessed the work God had done in her and her mother's lives over the past year. They were living in transitional housing. Mom was working, and baby Terea was thriving. It was a humbling reminder of God's care and concern for his created ones.

We saw God at work in our hearts and the lives of women and children. Those opportunities to participate in being God's heart and hands on Earth were long-lasting, life-changing, love-increasing lessons for us all.

Pat lived wide awake by listening for God, knowing his voice, and following his lead. Today, Pat is fully wide awake in heaven. Those of us who knew and loved her honor her life by living our own lives wide awake.

> *"Since this is the kind of life we have chosen, the life of the Spirit, let us make sure that we do not just hold it as an idea in our heads or a sentiment in our hearts, but work out its implications in every detail of our lives" (Galatians 5:25 The Message).*

Pay Attention Practice One

We don't always get to know the story behind the mission, event, plan or program. I asked Heidi to give us that insight to show us what Pat modeled for her; listening to God on a walk, listening as she spent time with the Living Word, listening to stories in her own neighborhood, letting go of a really good program that had a good life, and paying attention for what would be next. To live wide awake is to pay attention to the Holy Spirit, to what is going on around us and to respond. In this story, Pat's response rippled out to another leader Heidi Hoback, to a team of mothers and daughters and into the lives of many God sent us to love on.

Start with a blank piece of paper. Read Galatians 5 slowly today and record words and phrases that are:

emphasized,
repeated,
relatable,
similar,
significant,
surprising,
or stand out.

You will end up with a full page. Choose one of the words or phrases to pay attention to today. Here's how to 'pay attention':

Repeat it to yourself through the day.
Talk to someone else about it.
Do something about it.
Ask God why it stood out to you.

Read before or after the chapter - putting the words in larger context.

Look for where the word or phrase intersects your circumstances.

Look up where that word or phrase is used in other parts of the Living Word.

Pay Attention Practice Two

Read Galatians 5 out loud or listen to it.

Asking questions reminds us that we don't know everything. Approach today's practice by telling God you are sorry for the pride of acting like you do know it all sometimes. Ask for forgiveness and enter this space humbly and eagerly to see how questions reveal our dependence. Remember, God is knowable, but God is mysterious. We will never know everything about anything. Let the tension of unknowing keep you humble, keep you curious, and keep you coming to the Word.

Let yourself wonder and ask questions based on listening to Galatians 5. Make a list of questions beginning with these words. Sit in these questions today: How, When, Why, What, Where, I wonder.

Examples: What can I do differently?
How do I/How do we find favor with God?

Pay Attention Practice Three

I grew up in the church thinking that the only people who shared the Good News about Jesus were missionaries who heard a specific call to go to a country outside the USA where there were people who had not yet heard of Jesus. People in our church had a photo of missionaries we supported hanging on our refrigerator. The missionaries would visit our church once in a while and get about five minutes to tell us what they were doing. I thought most of them went to China or Africa.

When I got older, I thought "doing ministry" was for people who were hired by a church or non-profit, faith-based organization. Thankfully, I have learned those things are only partly true. True, being a missionary is a calling. True, being employed by a church is a job where work is to care for the gathering of people inside the church. However, there are people everywhere who have not heard of Jesus--and in fact, many are right here in the USA. Some are sitting in churches. Some people have heard about Jesus and still have questions. They might live next door, sit next to you in class, or work with you.

Pat Jones was one of the people who showed me what it meant to be the church outside the building--for the church isn't just a building with an address. The church is people loved by God eating, drinking, volunteering, hiking, painting, fundraising together. The church is a combination of people who know God and who are searching for God who are hat-making, party-throwing, baby rocking, hand-holding, foot washing, weed-pulling, house building, and funeral attending.

The church inside the building is dynamic. People move, programs end, pews get exchanged for chairs. Leadership shifts, focus shifts, service times and styles shift. There are endings and beginnings. Endings deserve a celebration of what was. Endings mean change, and change = loss. Endings also deserve time for us to grieve what is not the same anymore. Beginnings are bumpy. They deserve time to be messy so they can someday become marvelous. Pat modeled what it looks like to end well and begin anew. She invited so many to take the love of God and live it wide awake both messy and marvelous.

Anyone who knows Jesus gets to share the good news wherever they are and when necessary, use words. Most commonly, we all can do what Pat did: listen for God's voice, follow God's lead, and go love whatever part of the world we're in. That mission is always possible.

Read Galatians 5:1
Write this out in your own words as a type of mission statement or life purpose or life-long goal.

Read Galatians 5: 3-6, 13-15, 26
Everyone faces obstacles that deflect us from living wide awake, living as people set free. Do you recognize what your obstacles are? Stop for a few moments, close your eyes and ask the Holy Spirit to help you see your own handicaps and stumbling blocks. Thank the Spirit for the insight, then write them down. Put a circle around each one and slash through the circle as a visual of your obstacles being overcome or removed or healed as the Spirit sets us free.

Read Galatians 5:25
This is the key to living wide awake! Personalize this verse, use your creativity, make it your own, make it memorable.

What can you and God do together to love the world?

Pay Attention Practice Four

One evening after dinner at my friend Adie's house, I was standing at the counter putting food in containers. I asked her if she liked her new Bosch dishwasher. She told me it was the best she had ever had. Her favorite part was how quiet it was. She said, "Can you hear it? Because it's on right now."

I was leaning up against the handle and, because I heard absolutely nothing, I didn't believe it was on. She told me to open it up. Sure enough, the spray of hot soapy water stopped as I pulled the door open. The working dishwasher was silent.

The dishwasher was doing the work it does without anyone hearing it, seeing it, or being aware it was even working. This is my favorite way to think about the work of the Holy Spirit. The Spirit is at work. The results of the dishwasher were evident when the work was complete, and so the work of the Spirit is seen, partly, in healed people, in transformed lives, in the beauty of creation. And someday, it will be seen completed.

> *Trust God from the bottom of your heart;*
> *don't try to figure out everything on your own.*
> *Listen for God's voice in everything you do,*
> *everywhere you go;*
> *He's the one who will keep you on track.*
> *Don't assume that you know it all*
> *(Proverbs 3: 5 The Message).*

Read Galatians 5:16-26 in your own Bible and in The Message.

Take two pages of paper. In the center of one put this title: Living My Way. Fill the page with what Galatians describes as following the desires of your sinful nature or desires of the flesh. Sin is a condition affecting our wholeness and shows up in the ways we behave and believe that are contrary to the holiness of God. Next, get specific with reflecting on your own life. What are the ways your heart, mind, and will turn you away from the direction of loving God?

Though this practice might bring up strong feelings or a quick sense of defensiveness, I promise you, taking time for honest reflection and confession is refreshing. You face a patient King, a forgiving Saviour, a kind Prince of Peace. Do not be afraid.

At the center of the second page, put this title: Living Wide Awake. Fill the page with what the Holy Spirit produces in our life when we are convicted of our own junky behavior, confess it to Jesus, receive forgiveness, and surrender control.

When you're done with both pages, go back to the first one and draw a large cross over the top of it all, and write out Galatians 5:24 boldly on that page.

Pay Attention Practice Five

Listen to Galatians 5 or read it slowly.

Choose a verse or two to memorize it; that will help you live in the freedom Jesus Christ gave you. Write out the verse in a place you can return to easily. Use bright colored pens, do some hand lettering, or draw an image of freedom, loving the world, or listening to God's voice.

That is how we live wide awake.

Let the Word Work

Today, simply ask the Spirit to show you who and how to love. Live wide awake, paying attention, so you can follow where the Spirit leads. It may be a quiet nudge to encourage someone or a small act of kindness. You don't need to rely on what you understand. Trust the Spirit.

Going Deeper

If you are intrigued by the Holy Spirit, read what Jesus said at the end of his time here on Earth.

John 14:23-27
John 16:5-15

Approach the living word with gratitude and curiosity.

Engage by writing down your questions, beginning with "I wonder…"

Ask other people you interact with this week what they wonder about the Holy Spirit.

Thank Jesus for his representative--the Advocate--and all that is done for us through the ongoing work of the Spirit.

We had a ball-chasing, fence-crashing, long-distance-swimming labrador named Moses. He weighed in at just over 110 pounds. Nearly everyone we met commented on his handsomeness, then asked us if he was part Great Dane.

He was a gentle giant with small children, allowing them to pull on his ears and even grab at whatever he might have in his mouth. He loved tennis balls. You would throw and he would return it to you for as long as you were willing to touch the nasty, foam-covered thing.

A lot of exercise was required to keep this big boy well behaved. He was decent on the other end of the leash unless I came into the vicinity of another dog. Some other dogs caused him stress, which turned him from a confident, kind dog into an unpredictable one. He displayed protective behavior, sometimes aggressively. Because of this, I called a professional. We set up a time for the trainer to come to our house, with instructions to not feed him his morning meal and to not react to anything the dog would do when the trainer came to the house.

Dogs, especially food-motivated labradors, don't take kindly to not being fed. Moses was squirmy and overly-energetic when the trainer arrived. I answered the door and Moses gave him the big dog greeting of head, shoulder, knees, and toes body-to-body love. The trainer didn't respond to one single thing the dog did. Instead, he started talking to me, introducing himself and reminding me not to speak, touch, or correct Moses at all.

For at least thirty minutes this man discussed dog behavior, goals of training, how people need to send the right messages to dogs, the fine points of pack behavior, and me needing to be a confident leader of the pack rather than the dog. Never once did he even glance at Moses, who eventually gave up his many varied attempts to get this man's attention.

Moses was still hungry and did what he could to remind me. The trainer told me he was going to take out a freeze dried raw food patty, make it wet, and put it in Moses's dog bowl. Again, I was instructed to stand off to the side and not react. Without saying anything, the trainer turned toward Moses with the bowl in hand and pointed a finger at Moses's rear end. That dog sat down. Then the trainer began to slowly lower the bowl of deliciousness to the floor. Moses stood up and moved right to it. The trainer pulled up the bowl. Moses sat, but when the bowl lowered again, Moses stood, head lurching toward that overdue breakfast. The bowl got pulled up again.

Moses started panting, sitting, laying down, whining, and walking in circles, drool lengthening on each side of his mouth. Each time he stopped and sat the bowl would be slowly lowered to the floor, but any time he moved the bowl would be brought up to its starting position. No words were ever used, only the finger pointing at the back end of the hungry dog. I found myself holding my breath, feeling the frustration. But finally the bowl went lower and the dog stayed put. The bowl made it to the floor and the trainer took his hands off and stood back up. Moses' eyes were glued to the man's face. With his finger pointing to the bowl, one confidently-spoken word came out of the trainer's mouth directed at Moses: "Release."

One well-timed sentence followed that, directed at me: "You want him to know that all good things come from his master."

Moses hesitated slightly, then bowed his head and inhaled the freeze dried meat. I cried.

I thought, isn't that exactly the way of my Master Jesus? He too wants me to know that all good things come from His hand. At my core, I too am so hungry for His provision, for the certainty of knowing He is aware of my condition and will meet my needs.

The trainer then went on to talk to me about leading Moses in a way that would allow the dog to trust me to be his leader. He will look to me for calm direction and feel confident I would satisfy his needs and help him navigate challenges. I would learn to kindly ask him to repeatedly obey me. We were establishing a relationship of trust. The lesson was not lost on me, but certainly went beyond what was supposed to happen between me and my dog.

Bob Goff posted this thought on Instagram one day and it sounded similar to what the dog trainer said:

"Live in constant anticipation of God's good pleasure."

Paul wrote something in Romans that lines up with Bob and the dog trainer.

> *"This resurrection life you received from God is not a timid, grave-tending life. It's adventurously expectant, greeting God with a childlike, "What's next, Papa?"*
> *(Romans 8: 15 The Message).*

I read the Living Word as a call to Live Wide Awake. Wide awake people pay attention, are willing to show up, trust and participate with what the Master is doing. They engage as genuinely as possible, drawing resources from the One who loves.

In the time you spend in the Word this week, I pray you find what you are most hungry for. May the Word lead you to both anticipate and trust that all the best of life is God's good pleasure. He's pouring it out on you, on the world. Receive it. Praise Him. Let it work its way through your ordinary, everyday life as you live wide awake.

Pay Attention Practice One

Pray these words of Paul from Ephesians 1:18-20 prior to your reading today.

> *"Ask the God of our Master, Jesus Christ, the God of glory—to make you intelligent and discerning in knowing him personally, your eyes focused and clear, so that you can see exactly what it is he is calling you to do, grasp the immensity of this glorious way of life he has for his followers, oh, the utter extravagance of his work in us who trust him—endless energy, boundless strength!"*

Today you will be reading a meaty and meaningful chapter in the book called Romans. I suggest you read it in your own Bible and The Message which speaks with fresh, relevant voice. The Message paraphrase has given me a deeper understanding and appreciation of Romans.

Everything good comes from a perfectly good God. List or underline every good gift you find in Romans 8.

Who are the people, where are the places, what are the behaviors or activities you go to when you need something,
when you're anxious or afraid,
when you feel fragile,
when things are changing,
when you lose control,
when you're unhappy, or
when you've blown it?

If God is for you, how will you live in your everyday life?

Pay Attention Practice Two

My Bible Study Fellowship teaching leader said something that hit me hard. I've never forgotten.

"There is a battle going on, and the consequences are life or death. The battle is over your mind."

Candy VanArk

Imagine yourself in a room full of people who are being prepared to go fight an enemy together. A highly trained, brilliant, and experienced five-star general is about to explain exactly what is going on in terms you can understand. What he is about to say is vital. He lays out the tactics of the enemy clearly. He knows the overwhelming power of the Holy Spirit and presents overwhelming hope. You are paying close attention because your life depends on listening, learning, and living as if it is true.

Romans 8:1-18. Listen to it or read it out loud so you can hear what is being said as if the general was speaking it.

Read the passage again, then create your own visual image of the battle that is going on.

Read a third time and choose a verse or your own summary to help you remember what this part of Romans is about.

Pay Attention Practice Three

Read Roman 8: 18-30 out loud so you can hear what is being said.

Think of all the people you know who are physically ill, suffer with mental illness, struggle with relationships, addictions, disabilities, finances, or loneliness. Close your eyes and see these people in front of you. Imagine what it looks like as every one of them is set free from the death and decay that causes their brokenness.

Read the passage again.

Write out verses 26 through 28. Use them to have a conversation with God. Ask for wisdom to understand His will and the faith to trust His purposes and promises.

Or use this time to speak honestly about your lack of trust, your reasons for doubt, or what is making your heart hard.

Or spend time thanking God for the promise that the details of your life and those you thought about today are worked into God's perfect plan.

Pay Attention Practice Four

Romans 8:31-38
Divide a piece of paper in half vertically. On the left, make a list of the questions being asked in your own words.

On the right, record the answers to the questions.

Read Romans 8: 31-38 again with the goal of finding the most significant verses.

Pay Attention Practice Five

Read Romans 8 slowly.

What are the truths in this passage that can help you live wide awake instead of in fear or isolation, instead of being bound by doubt, discouragement, or demanding your own way, instead of holding on to anger, hate, or bitterness, instead of drowning in anxiousness, despair, or shame?

Claim every good thing, every truth--speak them out loud. Write each one down and date when you wrote it.

Finish this time in prayer, on your knees, praising Father, Son, and Spirit for loving you like this. If you feel convicted, recommit to living your life wide awake in the power and love of the life-giving Spirit.

Let the Word Walk

Remember, everyone needs the good news and good things you read about this week. The Spirit of God in us is giving life, offering forgiveness, bringing peace and loving the world he created like crazy. Look for your opportunity to share with at least one person what you discovered this week about our trustworthy Master.

Go Deeper

Read through another chapter of Romans, recording what is significant to you, the questions you have, and what is true. Record what you don't want to forget.

Here are a few I would suggest and a sneak peek of their message:

Romans 3
God's fairness and faithfulness
What is true of all people?
What is true for everyone who believes?

Romans 5
Peace with God
Relationship with God
Grace of God...all because of Jesus

Romans 6
Spoiler alert: death gets crushed and
you get a new life

Romans 11
Mercy Mercy Mercy

Fear Knots

On March 17, 2003, I was sitting at a conference for speakers and writers in Florida. My purpose for being there was to learn how to be a keynote speaker. "I'm not a writer," I repeated throughout the week. When the focus was on writing, I tuned it out. How much can one person absorb in a three-day conference?

One morning was devoted to listening for seeds of interest that we might develop as topics for our own speaking or writing. The morning began with a line of well-seasoned speakers and authors who, one by one, shared their areas of expertise. Following that large group session, we, the conference attendees, would return to our smaller groups to give an impromptu talk on the seed of interest we might develop and why. We were listening to people, but were also meant to be listening for the Spirit to prompt us. As the line of speakers and authors who were sharing got smaller and smaller and my page was empty of any seeds, I decided to override listening to the speakers and write down a generic topic so I wouldn't go back into my small group seedless.

While trying to come up with a simple something, the Spirit spoke these two words to me: "Fear and anxiety."

Immediately I spoke these two words back: "No thanks."

I tried more guessing, but "fear and anxiety" repeated over and over. I asked what in the world I knew about fear and anxiety. The question was directed at God, and he answered quickly, specifically:

People, situations, even my very own fears flooded my thoughts and completely drowned out everything else that was happening in that Florida conference room.

I had a Fear Knot (also known as a panic attack), on the way back to the room with my small group. In order to delay the horrible three minutes when I would have to speak with virtually no preparation, I volunteered to go find toilet paper for the women's bathroom. They were dangerously low. Looking for the janitor and solving the TP crisis made me the last one to get to the small group room. We were seated for less than a minute when my name was called to speak first. Of course. Do you know it's possible to talk without breathing?

I spoke about how unnerving it was to have fear and anxiety be the seed of interest that chose me. I told a funny story illustrating my own anxiety, breaking my pent up tension about speaking without being prepared and not appreciating my topic. The rest of the nervous presenters laughed with relief.

Later that night in my hotel room, I watched the news. The top story was President Bush having just given Saddam Hussein forty-eight hours to leave the country or there would be war.

The morning of March 18, 2003, our main speaker started the first session with these words: "The world shares a universal emotion today: Fear." Oh great. So my seed of interest apparently appealed to the whole world. I might not like it, but clearly it was universally relatable.

This quote about the best topics speakers and writers use, was on the workbook page next to the place I wrote down the dreadful seed of mine:

"There is very probably something in my background that most everyone in the audience can relate to. I am no longer just the speaker to those listeners; I am a person with whom they have something in common."

Carolyn Warner

So, huh, well…ok. Thanks for that, Carolyn, but I'm not a writer.

Ten years later…

I am a writer. You are reading something that I wrote. I can relate to nearly all the quirks and obstacles writers deal with. The hardest one: getting my butt in the chair to write. The next hardest: believing I have something to write that anyone wants to read. Ten years after I got the fear and anxiety seed of interest, I started researching and writing about it. I've also done a thirty-day blog about food as a love language. I've written an Advent booklet, made a dent in a novel, and finally finished this spiritual formation devotional. What amazes me is the way Jesus would lead me to a place I didn't consider going myself, a path I resisted heading down, a task I felt unqualified for. There continues to be healing of complex fear knots that have required hard work, repentance, and release. Jesus is doing in me what is impossible for me to do on my own. I am certain that is how he works in us and through us all.

Pay Attention Practice One

Read Matthew 14
A lot happens in this chapter. Take the time to write down a general timeline of events.

Next, write down points on the line where Jesus is doing something for or through others they could not do for themselves. The idea is to see the big picture, break it down, then bring it all back together.

Outlining details will help you remember and give you reference points.

Pay Attention Practice Two

Matthew 14: 1-14
Imagine you are a local journalist and have been invited to exclusively cover the birthday party of the year. You know the background of Herod's relationship to John and the scandal of Herod marrying his brother's wife, Herodias. "For Herod had arrested and imprisoned John as a favor to his wife Herodias (the former wife of Herod's brother, Philip)"

(See Luke 3:19-20 for further context of this party)

Read verses 1-12. Write down all the questions you can think of to ask Herod, his family, and guests about what happened at this party. Asking questions helps us slow down, dig deeper, and think about the story from a fresh perspective.

Was there anything new you saw in this story because of questions you asked?

Pay Attention Practice Three

Matthew 14: 12-21
Sit, kneel, or bow quietly and be present to the presence of God. Ask for anything you need today prior to reading His word (comfort, calm, focus, encouragement, energy, etc.).

Stay in the mindset of a journalist who is watching Jesus' interactions and listening to what He is saying. Read verses 12-14. Observe Jesus' responses to the news about John.

Read verses 15-21, paying attention to Jesus. How does he interact with the crowd, the disciples, his Father? What do you learn about Jesus from observing? What does he care about?

Is there anything you believe Jesus has asked of you that seems impossible for you to do? If so, bring it to him now.

Pay Attention Practice Four

This is my favorite story in the Living Word. I want to walk on water without experience, without water-walking shoes. I want the courage, faith, and pure devotion of a disciple trained to do exactly what he sees his Master doing. Those wants of mine come in waves. All the waves of doubt and distraction put me underwater, too. If you didn't know already, Peter doesn't drown. I've gotten tossed around, but haven't drowned either.

Read Matthew 14:22-36 from the perspective of Jesus. Write down your observations.

Read Matthew 14: 22-36 from the perspective of Peter. Write down your observations.

Read Matthew 14: 22-36 from the perspective of a disciple who stayed on the boat. Write down your observations.

NOTE: Observations can be who, what, where, when, how, why, or "I wonder" questions. Observations can be insights into the God of love and the love of God. Observations can be how the world you live in and your life circumstances seem to have a connection to what is happening in the story.

Observations come from paying attention to what is being said. You will glean information, but the purpose of engaging with the Living Word is also for transformation. Listen to the Master's message. It could change your day, or change your life.

Pay Attention Practice Five

"The Gospel is like a caged lion. It does not need to be defended, it just needs to be let out of its cage"

Charles Spurgeon

If you believe in a perfectly good and loving God, what do you think he wants from you? What do you think he wants for you?

One young woman I met said God wanted us to tell other people about him so they would go to church. I asked her to personalize what she said. She answered, "I think God would want me to tell my coworkers about my faith." I appreciated her honest answer.

I asked her if she thought the outcome of sharing her faith was so those people would go to church. She said yes. I asked her, what if God just wanted her to tell her coworkers about her own relationship to Jesus, her own story of faith, without the expectation they would go to church? She said, "Well, that would make it a whole lot easier." I told her that I would take that expectation and get rid of it for her. She was relieved.

There are all kinds of fear knots people who go to church, read their Bibles, and call themselves Christians have, that keep them from showing or telling others about the God of love and the love of God. I want to say to every fellow lover of Jesus: you are ready and able to live wide awake. You know your own story. You know God the way you know Him today, and next year you might know Him more. You don't need special training or all the answers. Don't 'should' on yourself with some unnecessary, made up expectation you think

God has dumped on you. The Spirit changes hearts. We get to tell the story.

Matthew 10 is an example of real people with real names who knew Jesus for less than 3 years. They probably had some Scripture memorized because there were no printed Bibles, but they had not made the cut for Rabbi school. They did ordinary family business before they followed Jesus all over the place. They were learning as they lived. Apparently, Jesus thought they were ready and able because one day, He sent them all out to tell the story.

Put yourself in the story as one of those young people who Jesus called to circle up because he had a purpose and a plan for them.

Read Matthew 10
As if you were taking notes in class, write down the key points you need to hear and remember. Write down your objections and "what if" questions.

As you listen to Jesus's words as one of the young people in the group, is there anything that makes you anxious or afraid?

Is something in your current circumstance causing you to be anxious or afraid?

What does Jesus say loud and clear to these young adults?

What is Jesus's strategy?

What is the message you need to hear?

Let The Word Walk

Report to someone what you saw and heard in this chapter just like a journalist would.

Go Deeper

Choose one of these activities:

1. Set a chair across from the one you are sitting in. See Jesus sitting there. With words of praise and thanks, acknowledge his kindness, love, miracles, and actions toward the people you read about in Matthew 14 this week, and toward you.

2. Talk to Jesus as if you have pulled him aside after hearing what he had to say in Matthew 10. Ask Jesus every question you have. Listen as you live for His response to your questions.

3. Write a letter to Jesus using words of praise and thanks. Acknowledge his kindness, love, miracles, and actions toward the people you read about in Matthew 14 this week, toward other people you know, and toward you.

Cheap Life Lessons

On my third pass stomping from the garage, through the laundry room where my mother was calmly ironing my hubby's shirts, down the hall and into the kitchen, I was sighing, slamming, and swearing. My mother finally asked, "What's wrong?"

Clearly, something was wrong.

"I lost my driver's license. I have looked everywhere, dumped out my purse, checked every pocket possible and stuck my finger under the seats, around the seats and even in the seat cracks where no fingers should have to go. I do not have time for a lost license. Do you know how awful it is to get a new one? I have no idea where else to look."

My calm mother, still running the hot iron back and forth over JR's thirty-fifth shrink and wrinkled work shirt, asked, "Did you pray about it?"

Did I PRAY about it?

What kind of a question is that--did I pray about a lost driver's license? As if Jesus wants to have a conversation with anyone about their silly little inconvenience.

No, actually, I didn't.

But then I did.

I went in the bathroom, which adjoined the laundry room where my wise mother ironed. I flushed the toilet, turned on the water and washed my hands. And I talked to Jesus. The prayer may have taken on an embarrassed, whiny, somewhat desperate tone. But I prayed.

The fourth time into the garage, I opened the back door again, laid my hand under the driver's seat again and set it on top of the driver's license--I am not kidding. I cried. When I came in the house crying my mom asked again, "What's wrong?" And with tears, I showed her the little plastic card.

"So why are you crying?" My calm mother asked.

"Because I can't believe God cares enough about something so insignificant, I can't believe he would answer my belligerent plea for help and I didn't even think to ask until you told me to, which I thought was silly at first, I didn't even *go* to the bathroom," I replied in one breath.

Eye rolling would have been justified, but my mom smiled and reminded me that God wants us to talk to Him about everything, anything, anytime, anywhere.

I wasted a big dose of worry, but the Lord didn't waste that experience. I have not forgotten how I felt seen by God and responded to immediately, even with my crappy attitude. That cheap life lesson demonstrated tangibly His care of my basic needs. If He cares about the insignificant, He certainly cares about what matters most.

I'm still prone to dramatic frustration and door slamming, though much less so than years ago. I continue to experience God being trustworthy in the minutiae and the mountains of living. I am quicker to go to prayer than to go ballistic when inconvenienced or interrupted by the unexpected. Though I struggle with anxiety, I keep showing up first thing in the morning to talk to Jesus, to look for His best for me, and to listen for what He needs me to hear.

Pay Attention Practice One

Luke 11: 1-13
Disciples asked Jesus to teach them to pray. Disciples would have done exactly what they saw and heard their Rabbi doing immediately after he did it. Disciples learned from their Rabbi by doing what he did, by listening, pondering, and deciding if they wanted to.

Eugene Peterson explains Luke 11 as the "primary text, (backed up by the Psalms) for guiding Christians into a life of personal, honest, and mature prayer." He points out this is Jesus's first and only lesson in prayer, and it is both short and simple. Prayer is a conversation between humans and God, and is the "act in which we move beyond ourselves...we come to be formed and defined not by the subtotal of our experiences, but by the Father, Son, and Spirit to whom and by whom we pray."[20]

Read Luke 11:1-13
Who is in this story and what is said about them?
Where does it take place?
When does it take place?
What do the people in the story say?
What is the point of the story?
Why was this story included (dig below the surface for meaning)?

Do you believe prayer matters? Do you believe prayer makes a difference? Do you pray as a last resort or a first response?

What are your qualifications for what your pray about?
Is prayer more than words?

Pay Attention Practice Two

My mom is a woman who has prayed all her life. She didn't tell me how; she showed me. It was ordinary for me and my four siblings to see our mom at the dining room table with her Bible open, a notebook next to that, and a devotional book on the other side. She had lists of people she prayed for. I was guilty of interrupting those morning prayers when I was getting ready for school and didn't know where my favorite jeans were. I can still find her on her knees or at her table doing the same things today. She is close to Jesus because she draws near daily. She doesn't do anything fancy; she speaks to God with praise and thanksgiving, by asking questions, making requests, and listening. She also lives prayer in trusting that God sees, the Spirit leads, and Jesus gives her joy and strength to carry out her ordinary tasks in her everyday life. She lives as if the Spirit is praying on behalf of us all, and as if God knows and wants and does what is best for His people all the time. She may not appreciate all this attention in writing, but I want you to get a glimpse because not everyone has seen prayer modeled. There is a lot to be said for learning from someone who lives prayer, versus learning about prayer from a sermon, a class, or a couple of books.

I asked her if she would share her thoughts on her experience with her Father. I am going to share advice from her experience with you for you to engage with. The first is my favorite.

My favorite Mother Mary advice: "*Ask Him to help you love to pray.*"

Today read another account of Jesus teaching us how to pray. Jesus is teaching, don't miss that. This time Matthew tells the same story. To get a taste of this teaching in our language, please read this in The

Message. It is dynamic and might clear up some misconceptions you have about praying.

Read Matthew 6: 1-18
Write down what words or phrases stand out to you. Did anything trip you up? Did you have a strong reaction to anything Jesus said? Is there a fresh perspective you gain by reading Matthew's version of Jesus's teaching?

What is the big idea you can apply to your life?

Pay Attention Practice Three

Naomi's Prayer

Naomi is my niece. When she was nine years old she told me matter-of-factly that if you just don't know how to pray, put your hands together and hold them next to your heart, thumbs touching your chest. Let your thumbs remind you to pray for people you love the most, those closest to your heart. Let your pointer finger remind you to pray for people who you would point to, like your good friends and important people in your life. Your tallest finger is a reminder to pray for those who are high in power and authority, like police, firefighters, and people who run the government, companies, and schools. Your ring finger is the weakest and reminds you to pray for people who are weak and suffering, like people who recently had a hurricane destroy their city. The pinky finger reminds us to pray for people that we don't even know but have needs, too.

Jesus emphasized simplicity when it comes to praying. Naomi gets it. This is an effective way to bring ourselves, our neighbor, and the world nearer to the God of love.

Matthew 6
Read this whole chapter slowly, using your favorite translation. Make two columns on a piece of paper. At the top of one side, write: "Don't Do That." List all of the 'do not's' in this chapter. Jesus is pointing at what we might be doing that isn't what is best for our relationship with him, with ourselves, or with others. He also gives a command to do something else in place of the do nots. Write "Do This" at the top of your second column. List what He says is important to do.

Mother Mary: "*Intercede, groan, weep for others. Tell Jesus what you desire, but ask Him to give you what is best for you. Interceding is talking to Jesus about what we or others lack. We don't have to persuade Him, we just have to tell him.*

If you have told someone you will pray for them, please do it. It seems to me a great offense to say you will but not do it."

Pay Attention Practice Four

If prayer is dull, easily avoidable, or feels like a duty, you're not alone. Many believers might be honest enough to admit they share that attitude toward prayer. Prayer may change for you once you realize the emphasis is on transformation, not transaction. What if you approached prayer willing to have a conversation with the Almighty--willing to participate in the healing and wholeness he is working into you?

I'm convinced my two-way ongoing conversation with God makes it possible for me to live wide awake. To live wide awake means to pay attention, participate, cooperate, and celebrate in an ongoing relationship of knowing and loving God.

I talk to God about what I want and why I want what I am asking for. Those conversations usually uncover underlying longing, underlying doubt, unasked questions, and a lack of understanding. Prayer is processing my life with the one who can listen forever, read between the lines, and hear beyond my current emotional state or messy words. When He speaks or acts in ways that look like answers, I am blown away by how well He knows me. I am reminded He does hear me. I am shown over and over that God cares about us, cares for us, and cares generously toward you and me.

Today I want to introduce you to a simple spiritual exercise taught by St. Ignatius of Loyola called Prayer of Examen. He encouraged people to talk to Jesus like a friend. You read several accounts of Jesus talking to friends in Luke 11 and Matthew 6. You are welcome to look up a more in-depth version of this, but simple is best. One of the unique parts of this pay attention practice is the emphasis on doing it at the end of the day. If you do it regularly, you'll find it an antidote to boredom and duty. The dullness will turn into developing a deep level of sensitivity to recognizing the presence of God and the movement of the Holy Spirit.

1. Sit quietly present to become aware of the presence of God.

2. Review the day with gratitude.
   Gratitude is the foundation of our relationship with God. Walk through your day in the presence of God and note its joys and delights.

3. Pay attention to your emotions.
   Reflect on the feelings you experienced during the day. Ask what God is saying through these feelings.

4. Choose one feature of the day and pray from it.
   Ask the Holy Spirit to direct you to something during the day that God thinks is particularly important. It may be a vivid moment or something that seems insignificant.

5. Look toward tomorrow.
   Ask God to give you light for tomorrow's challenges. End the Daily Examen with a conversation with Jesus. Ask forgiveness for your sins. Ask for his protection and help. Ask for his wisdom about the questions you have and the problems you face. Do all this in the spirit of gratitude.

Mother Mary: "*I, myself, pray because I cannot live without the results of prayer.*"

Pay Attention Practice Five

Luke 11: 1-2 and Matthew 6: 9-10
Jesus teaches us to use the name Father, including 'in heaven' and 'may your kingdom come.' I do often use an image of Jesus seated on a throne in a space that is bright and big and full of people, but not crowded.

What do you call the One you pray to?

I would like you to use your creative mind to wonder about what it looks like when you pray to your Father in heaven. I am going to ask some questions; you let an image come to mind. Remember, you were created with the ability to imagine. This might not be your cup of tea, but I promise this practice isn't scary or silly. It's sacred, and if you engage an image in your prayer, it will begin to expand your relationship and conversation with the Father.

What does a throne look like? Where is it--indoors, outdoors? What is around it? What do you notice about its size, color, material?

Notice Jesus walking toward it and seating himself on it. What does Jesus look like, seated on the throne? What expression is on his face? What is he wearing? Where is he looking?

Where are you in the space as you are observing? Are you seated, standing, lying down? How do you feel looking at Him on the throne? What are you thinking about? What do you want to do right now--go closer, say hello, hold His hand, sit by His feet? How do you feel being that close to His presence?

What is going on in your present circumstance that takes up a lot of your time or emotional energy? What can't you stop thinking about or trying to control, fix, figure out, or resolve? Imagine putting those people or situations in your two hands and move toward Jesus on His throne. Approach the throne with confidence; you will find mercy and grace for your need.

End this time with a prayer of awe and gratitude. Record your experience in your journal.

If something comes toward you with grace and can pass through you and toward others with grace, you can trust it as the voice of God.

It takes so much courage and humility to trust the voice of God within.

"We must learn how to recognize the positive flow and to distinguish it from the negative resistance within ourselves. It takes years of practice. If a voice comes from an accusation and leads to an accusation, it is quite simply the voice of the 'Accuser,' which is the literal meaning of the biblical word 'Satan.' Shaming, accusing, or blaming is simply not how God talks"

Richard Rohr[21]

Mother Mary: "*When you pray, kneel--it helps me realize who God is and who I am. Raise your hands to praise, hold them out to receive. Picture Jesus looking lovingly at you, smiling and so full of joy that you are praying to Him. Say at least some of your prayers out loud. Praise and thanksgiving are so important. I always begin and end with this.*"

Let the Word Walk

Choose a notebook, journal, or the pages provided to create a prayer list if you don't already have one. Here is a list to get you started:

People
Organizations
Current Events
The future
Yourself
Thanks
Questions
Surrender

Make a routine time in your day to pray through your list.

Going Deeper

When you are listening to someone share something rough, take the opportunity to pray with them at the end of the conversation. It might make you uncomfortable at first, and if you need to work your way up to this, begin by learning to ask, what can I specifically pray for you? If they don't have anything specific, pray over them and trust the Spirit to interpret.

Doing this is powerful. It's a gift. It's our privilege.

REFERENCES

Throughout entire book:

Scripture references from the New Living Translations
Tyndale. (2011). *NLT Study Bible*. Carol Stream, IL: Tyndale House Publishers.
Scripture references from The Message
Peterson, E. (2014). *The Message: The Bible in Contemporary Language*. Carol Stream, IL: Tyndale House.

A Note About Translations

[1] Peterson, E. H. (2009). In the company of translators. In *Eat This Book: A Conversation in the Art of Spiritual Reading* (p. 175). Grand Rapids, MI: Wm. B. Eerdmans Publishing.
[2] Peterson, E. H. (2009). In the company of translators. In Eat This Book: A Conversation in the Art of Spiritual Reading (p. 165). Grand Rapids, MI: Wm. B. Eerdmans Publishing.

Wildflowers and Roses

[3] New Living Translation (NLT)
Holy Bible, New Living Translation, copyright © 1996, 2004, 2015 by Tyndale House Foundation. Used by permission of Tyndale House Publishers, Inc., Carol Stream, Illinois 60188. All rights reserved.

Big Girl Pants

[4] Richard Rohr, an infectiously jovial, flannel-plaid-wearing Franciscan friar, with a childlike joy for telling the world that Jesus Christ loves everyone and is in everything. From Rohr, R. (2019, February 8). Seeing Christ Everywhere — Center for Action and Contemplation. Retrieved from https://cac.org/seeing-christ-everywhere-2019-02-13/

Know Who You're Not

[5] Ortberg, J. (2009). *Everybody's Normal Till You Get to Know Them*. Grand Rapids, MI: Zondervan.

[6] Glei, J. K., & Schwartz, T. (2013). Building a rock solid routine. In *Manage Your Day-To-Day: Build Your Routine, Find Your Focus, and Sharpen Your Creative Mind* (p. 51). Amazon.Com Publishing.
[7] Kim, M. (2019). I'm finally ready to talk about this. Retrieved from https://mikekim.com/theyear2016

Tell Me About Yourself

[8] From a Tuesday Teaching in the Hopewrites community that I am a member of, where Emily P Freeman was interviewing Annie F Downs.
Freeman, E. P. (2019). hope*writers. Retrieved from https://www.hopewriters.com
[9] Freeman, E. P. (2013). *A Million Little Ways: Uncover the Art You Were Made to Live* (pp. 200-201). Revell.

Peanut Butter Toast

[10] Peterson, E. H. (2014). Genesis. In *The Message: The Bible in Contemporary Language* (2nd ed., p. 24). Carol Stream, IL: Tyndale House.
[11] Stanley, A. (2016). Going Wide. In *Deep and Wide: Creating Churches Unchurched People Love to Attend* (p. 159). Grand Rapids, MI: Zondervan.
[12] Peterson, E. H. (2014). Genesis. In *The Message: The Bible in Contemporary Language* (2nd ed., p. 24). Carol Stream, IL: Tyndale House.

God Can Do Anything You Know

[13] Peterson, E. (2014). Isaiah 40. In *The Message: The Bible in Contemporary Language* (2.0th ed., p. 1092). Carol Stream, IL: Tyndale House.

Becoming A Mother

[14] Ortberg, J. (2014). Faith, doubt, and being born. In *Know Doubt: Embracing Uncertainty in Your Faith* (p. 23). Grand Rapids, MI: Zondervan.
[15] Douglas, J. D., & Tenney, M. C. (1989). Dictionary. In *NIV Compact Dictionary of the Bible* (1st ed., p. 427).

Oh You Love Me Like That

[16] Willard, D. (2009). *Knowing Christ Today: Why We Can Trust Spiritual Knowledge*. Grand Rapids, MI: Zondervan.
[17] Zondervan. (1987). John. In *Amplified Bible* (p. 13:34). Grand Rapids, MI: Author.
[18] Jr., M. R. (2016). *Invitation to a Journey: A Road Map for Spiritual Formation* (p. 19). Downers Grove, IL: InterVarsity Press.
[19] Angelou, M. (2010). *I Know Why the Caged Bird Sings*. New York, NY: Random House.

Cheap Life Lessons

[20] Peterson, E. H. (2009). Ears thou hast dug for me. In *Eat This Book: A Conversation in the Art of Spiritual Reading* (pp. 106-107). Grand Rapids, MI: Wm. B. Eerdmans Publishing.
[21] From Richard Rohr, *The Universal Christ: How a Forgotten Reality Can Change Everything We See, Hope For, and Believe* (Convergent: 2019), 87, 88-89.

Made in the USA
Monee, IL
23 February 2023

28287613R00154